HIGH OCTANE SELLING

HIGH OCTANE SELLING

Boost Your Creative Power to Close More Sales

Ray Anthony & Malcolm Kushner

Illustrations by David Bamberg

amacom
American Management Association
New York • Atlanta • Boston • Chicago • Kansas City • San Francisco • Washington, D.C.
Brussels • Mexico City • Tokyo • Toronto

Library of Congress Cataloging-in-Publication Data

Anthony, Ray
    High octane selling : boost your creative power to close more
sales / Ray Anthony & Malcolm Kushner : illustrations by David
Bamberg.
        p.   cm.
    Includes bibliographical references.
    ISBN 0-8144-7898-0
    1. Selling. I. Kushner, Malcolm L. II. Title.
HF5438.25.A58   1995
658.85—dc20   95-21036
                                                               CIP

Printing number

10 9 8 7 6 5 4 3 2 1

To High Octane Professionals

This book is dedicated to those innovative, light-hearted, and courageous salespeople who are not afraid to make a valiant creative effort and fail. But who, in the end, through their imagination, tenacity, and healthy sense of humor about life, ultimately succeed to find a vastly superior way to sell and service their customers. And to whom "great" just isn't good enough.

Contents

Foreword

Are you like me? Do you hate self-improvement books? They're so . . . wonky. Plus that nasty implication that I could improve!

High Octane Selling doesn't do that. It's more like a world-improvement book, as in "the world would be better (have more fun, pay more attention) if I could just invoke my world-class creativity (or at least rip off some of the great ideas in this book)."

I have neckties older than some of the people I compete with today. Combine that sorry fact with my most consistent behavioral trait—laziness—and right away you can see that I need help. Forget the level playing field. I want a downhill tilt, a tailwind, and compromising photos of the referee. Actually, those are not what I want most in life. What I want most in life is to maximize my emotional bank account (my EBA). To have fun. To extend myself for others. And to win.

What I love about *High Octane Selling* is that it pulls all of my EBA levers: I had fun reading it—it's a funny book—so just read it. Even if you give it away when you're done, you'll be better off than if you hadn't read it. But not as well off as if you read it and try some of the stuff.

Lots of the ideas in here will draw you out, and have you stretching yourself, doing things that will be really good for your customers, your colleagues, your boss. You'll grow and so will they.

"Winning isn't everything, it's the only thing." Duh. Is there anyone here who would prefer not to win? "Sorry, sir. Wrong book." Wrong planet, in fact.

Over my (blush) thirty-year sales career, I find that winning does more for my EBA than losing. Winning's better for my FBA too.

Twenty-three years ago, I sold my way out of low-tech into

high-tech by landing a sales job at Digital Equipment Corporation. Difficult, since they only hired computer whizzes and I stood on a rubber mat to change my flashlight batteries. But I got to the top guy by offering him a free ride to the airport and littering my car seats with borrowed computer books so he'd ask me why. So I could tell him how bad I wanted the job, how hard I'd work for him, and of course the books were part of the message.

Today I work at Silicon Graphics, but I'm still a low-tech guy in a high-tech world. I am the Joe D. on pages 6 and 66. That's where you can learn how I used multimedia to dazzle a frazzled General Motors exec and open him up. I used it like an electronic Rolodex, popping up video clips of GM engineers and supporters elsewhere who had firsthand experience with Silicon Graphics' products. Someday, that will be common, but it wasn't in May 1993, and it still packs a wallop.

Creativity—doing something remarkable, unexpected— gets noticed. Add some relevant humor and you cannot miss. Impossible. The target will be engaged, charmed, intrigued, delighted. Remember that GM executive I mentioned? He was due at an urgent meeting called by his CEO! He skipped it, stayed with me, heard the Silicon Graphics message. He skipped the bucket brigade that day to check out the new fire engine. Creativity opened doors.

The cornball free-ride with books for the Digital sales manager landed me a job that started a career of differentiated selling. Stand-out work. I've gotten CEO's and auditoriums of 2,000 people to stand and recite limericks, pledging to some goal or product. I've kicked off seminars with a 4-minute video of a 1965 drive across Paris flatout in a Ferrari, without police escort or special effects. To get their hearts pumped so they'd pay attention.

Product specs? Who cares? Like oxygen and water, essential but hardly sufficient for a satisfying life.

Let me ask you a question: What was the most significant thing you've ever done professionally? I'll bet it required innovation and a challenge to the status quo. And how did it feel? How'd the old emotional bank balance move *that* day?

Treat yourself to the buffet of ideas here from Ray and Malcolm. Like the old Rowan and Martin "Laugh-In," even if you hit one you hate, just turn the page for the next jewel.

And try some. Just because you are a sales professional doesn't mean you can't have a lot of fun. Just keep making it *look* hard.

—Joe DiNucci, Vice President, Manufacturing
    Industries at Silicon Graphics Computer Systems, Inc.

What This Book Is About

Is looking inside a refrigerator the only way you can get a lightbulb to go on over your head? Then this is the book for you. Because successful selling in the 1990s and beyond requires one thing that's more important than good products or good services—good ideas!

Have you ever had an idea that closed a sale? An inspiration that overcame a tough objection? A revelation that generated a referral? A flash of insight that turned a prospect into a customer? Good. Because in today's increasingly competitive sales environment, your success will require many more ideas!

The old tricks don't work anymore, and you can't get by on a smile and a shoeshine. Even in-depth product or service knowledge isn't enough. Today's customers are more sophisticated than ever before. If you want their business, you've got to be creative. And that's where *High Octane Selling* comes in.

We have written this book for one purpose and one purpose only: to help you realize your full potential as a sales professional. That means tapping your own creativity to:

- ✪ Generate more leads.
- ✪ Recognize opportunities before your competitors do.
- ✪ Increase your income.
- ✪ Make your customers happy beyond their wildest dreams.
- ✪ Close more sales.

When you learn to harness the power of creativity, there is no boundary to what you can achieve. After all, the only limit is your own imagination!

Sure, you can read other books that claim to reveal the secret of sales success. You can sell strategically, consultatively, or cybernetically. You can overcome objections, ram through road blocks, or attack like a guerilla. You can develop a magnetic personality or dress for success. You can also stand on your head and spit wooden nickels. By the time you're done, you won't know if you're opening or closing or coming or going. And, bottom line: Sales techniques are useful, but sales *ideas* are crucial!

And that's what *High Octane Selling* is all about: how to get ideas that will improve your sales performance. The book will introduce you to basic concepts in creativity and how to apply them in real-life sales situations. You will learn how to view problems from a fresh perspective, develop new paths around old obstacles, transform your intuition into a powerful sales tool, and develop breakthrough ideas in all aspects of selling. The emphasis is on practical, easy-to-apply methods that you can start using today.

And please, don't fall for the old myth that you must possess a "special gift" for creativity. Baloney. Everyone is creative to varying degrees. You don't have to be an Einstein to become a more creative sales professional. Anyone can learn to tap the power of their natural creativity. All it requires is an average amount of curiosity and the discipline to apply a few simple techniques provided by this book.

Too busy to read a whole book? Don't worry. We've designed *High Octane Selling* with *your* time constraints in mind. The book is divided into easy-to-read, two-page segments. Each sement covers a different creativity topic and is packed with nuts-and-bolts information. You can read them separately or together in any order you wish. Want to get started quickly? Try the "Service Station" section at the back of the book. It's chock full of ideas, worksheets, and other tools that you can put into practice immediately.

Whether you're looking to complement the sales methods you already use, or find radically new ways to sell, *High Octane Selling* will speed you to your goal. There's just one catch. You have to apply the lessons in the book. Try some of the exercises and techniques. Find the ones that work for you. Remember, if you get only one good idea, it will pay for this book many times over. So get your head out of the refrigerator and start selling!

Acknowledgments

From Ray Anthony:
   I'd like to thank some very special people who have helped me with this book. To my wonderful parents, Tony and Toni, for their loving support of me in the authoring venture. To my "special edition," Peggy Addington, who encouraged me, whose imagination gave me rich ideas, and who made me break out into countless endorphin-boosting laugh fests. To Linda Wilkens, my friend, for her wonderful research work. And to so many others over the years who have believed in me and shared their ideas with me. Thank you and God bless you all.

From Malcolm Kushner:
   The following people must be thanked for their strength in the face of adversity—they had to listen to me talk about this book. Some kind of medal must go to my wife, Christine Griger, who listened longer and better than anyone (or was she faking it?). I'd also like to thank Sam Kushner, my son, who never listens at all (but what can you expect from a four-year-old?). Others who had their ears put into various states of disrepair include Hank Kushner, Helen Kushner, Amy Tamarkin, Heather Tamarkin, John Cantu, Norman Mitgang, Neil Baron, Craig Fox, Bob Reed, Loyd Auerback, Stu Silverstein, Rich Herzfeld, Clair Swann, Jack Burkett, Debra DeCuir, and Donna Bedford. Special thanks also go to Joe DiNucci, David Sohm, and James Harris III. C'mon! Let's give them all a round of applause—they deserve it.

The information contained in this book may be hazardous to your health; before starting any medical treatment, consult with your own physician; the opinions expressed herein do not necessarily reflect the positions of the station; shake well before using; slow to 80 on the turns; do not remove tag; anyone related to the authors or holding stock in companies owned or operated by them, in whole or in part, is ineligible; the program rules, regulations, benefits, and conditions of participation may change at any time, with or without notice; offer void where prohibited; not to be used with any other promotion; advance reservations are required; other restrictions may apply.

The mainspring of creativity appears to be the same tendency which we discover so deeply as the curative force in psychotherapy—man's tendency to actualize himself, to become his potentialities. By this I mean the directional trend which is evident in all organic and human life—the urge to expand, extend, develop, mature—the tendency to express and activate all the capacities of the organism, or the self.

—Carl Rogers, *On Becoming a Person*

If no one ever took risks, Michelangelo would have painted the Sistine floor.

—Neil Simon

HIGH
OCTANE
SELLING

What Is
High Octane
Selling?

high oc·tane sell·ing (hī ŏk′ tān sĕl′ lgn), n. 1. an optimum performance concept. 2. escape from the dull and ordinary. 3. way of doing what you've never done before in impressive ways you've never imagined. 4. method of seeing invisible opportunities. 5. radically new way to expand your selling options—a world without limits. 6. process to put more challenge, fun, and excitement into your selling. 7. cause-and-effect behavioral form resulting in happy, satisfied, and smiling customers. 8. possibility amplifier. 9. systematic process that fattens your wallet.

Creativity . . . ??

A higher court judge once said that defining *justice* was like trying to nail jello to a wall. *Creativity* is even tougher to define. It's like trying to nail jello to a judge. It's far easier to sense that something is creative than to explain it. Creativity elicits a "Wow . . . how unique!" reaction. When asked to define jazz, the great Louis Armstrong shot back, "Man if you gotta ask you'll never know." Creativity is like that.

Creativity is essentially a process and behavior that produces novel and useful ideas. People get too hung up on thinking that something creative has to be "highly original." Actually every "new" idea is an outgrowth, modification, or synthesis of past ideas. "Originality" is a tricky concept too (just ask the Patent Office). Simply rearranging old things in wondrous new ways will produce effective surprises (just watch the "new" TV shows each fall). Creative can mean different, unconventional, nontraditional, or out-of-the ordinary.

Eddie G. was a dynamo of imagination. An automation equipment salesperson loved by his customers (executives at major New York City banks), he was a competent professional and a free spirit in a world of bland conformity. Having a flair for the dramatic, he would, after closing a sale, take a picture of himself drinking champagne from a silver slipper while his customers raised their flutes in celebration. He would then present them with a framed picture of the group as a memento. Different from shaking hands, wouldn't you agree? P.S.: His sales performance was consistently "sparkling."

"An idea is the most exciting thing there is."
—John Russell

Creative Selling
Is Deep in
His Soul

Joe D. is one of the most creative and successful sales executives in the computer industry. His techniques range from big-budget, flashy presentations to simple gestures that don't cost a dime. But they all have one thing in common—the customer never forgets them. Most people write sales letters. Not Joe. He sends videos. They're tailored to the prospect and very funny. One of his favorite gimmicks is filming himself singing a popular song with the lyrics changed to reflect his sales pitch. It doesn't win many Emmys, but it does win a lot of appointments.

The key is viewing things from the prospect's perspective. That's what Joe did when trying to sell computer workstations to Whirlpool executives. First he showed them a slide of his house. "This is my house," he noted. Then he showed a slide of a Whirlpool refrigerator in his kitchen, saying, "In every house there are great appliances." Then he showed a slide of his own company's workstation inside the refrigerator. "In every great appliance is a great workstation!" Joe enthusiastically announced. Surreal? Maybe. But Joe used it to dramatize a point: that his company sells workstations the same way Whirlpool sells refrigerators—based on quality, not just price. Another situation had Joe making his standard sales presentation. After the pitch the prospect mentioned that he liked Joe's tie. Immediately, Joe removed his tie and gave it to the man as a gift. "The guy loved it," recalls Joe. "He never stopped talking about it." And every time the fellow saw the tie in his closet, he thought of Joe. It was a small gesture that *tied* up a lot of business!

> **"How shall the soul of a man be larger than the life he has lived?"**
> **—Edgar Lee Masters**

Characteristics of Creative People

THE MANY FACES OF CREATIVITY

Creative people—artists, writers, scientists, entertainers, inventors, salespeople—share common traits and behaviors. Many are described on the following list. You need not possess all of them to be creative. But how many fit you?

Creative Salespeople. . . .

* Come up with lots of ideas quickly.
* Are flexible in their thinking styles.
* Tend to be emotional and intuitive.
* Work long, hard, and patiently in the pursuit of a challenging goal.
* Love solving tough problems, bringing order to chaos, and developing new opportunities.
* Get great joy expressing their creativity.
* Are widely informed on numerous highly diverse topics; have many different interests.
* Have a deep sense of curiosity about things.
* Take risks and are not afraid of failing.
* Persevere in spite of skepticism/criticism.
* Have a sense of humor (often "offbeat").
* Show a high tolerance for ambiguity.
* Tend to be very visually oriented.
* Are known as unconventional thinkers.
* Always want to improve things.
* Are confident they will eventually find solutions.
* Enjoy bending, stretching, or breaking rules.
* Feel they have a strong mission in life—a "destiny."
* Are playful and enjoy being "cutups."
* See things very "differently" than others.
* Are open-minded to new ideas and approaches.
* Love change, adventure, and an open and free environment to experiment with ideas.
* Are future-oriented, not past-focused.
* Think the "impossible" is often possible.

"Creative activity is one of the few self-rewarding activities. Being creative is like being in love."
—Woody Flowers

Irreplaceable, Not Indispensable

"No one is indispensable" has always been a maxim of business life. But don't despair. You can make yourself *irreplaceable!* Being irreplaceable means there's no substitute for the qualities and skills you bring to your position. Anyone else would be only a distant runner-up. You're like gold in a copper market. You're needed. You're valued. You're first choice. Your managers and customers don't want to lose you. Competitors wish you were in a different job.

One powerful and surefire way to make yourself irreplaceable is to *become as creative as you can.* Volunteer to tackle the toughest problems. Take on challenges others shrink from. Seek out and take advantage of opportunities everywhere. Foster change in yourself and others. Find ways to improve everything your sales organization does. *Be an innovator!* Then, you'll be totally irreplaceable and high above the crowd. You'll succeed faster and better than ever before.

Cynthia S. uses her creativity to lock in her customers' loyalty. She's set up joint brainstorming meetings between her company's support reps and her customer's staff to look for novel opportunities to use her products and services in niche customer applications. So far she's resourcefully helped her customers add $200,000 to their revenues. Ken H., her customer, told us, "Cynthia is immensely more than a 'salesperson.' She's our value-added creative consultant!" Cynthia's competitors shriek when they hear that she's been oh-so-creative again.

"Just as energy is the basis of life itself, and ideas the source of innovation, so is innovation the vital spark of all man-made change, improvement and progress."
—Theodore Levitt

Revving Up
Sales and Yourself

When you develop your innate creativity, you'll find that you can actually *revolutionize* the way you sell and service your customers. One sales manager aptly put it, "Why should I outspend or outwork my competitors when I can outsmart them instead?" Creativity will skyrocket your sales faster, better, and cheaper. The only limits to what you can do are those of your vast imagination. Sales productivity and effectiveness will blast through the roof.

Picture the toughest, most stubborn, and vexing sales problem or demanding objective confronting you. You've exhausted every conventional solution, approach, or strategy that you've learned in training or on the job. Nothing has worked. It seems hopeless and impossible. You feel totally at its mercy. You are about to give up and give in. What can you do?

Just pump some "premium" creative ideas into your think tank and watch newfound options turn into miracles. Creativity will open up areas of discovery and let you see and exploit rich invisible opportunities—new customers, market niches, and clever new uses for your product or service. You'll be able to eat your competitor's lunch anytime you select from the creativity menu.

While you're breaking old thinking habits, you'll be breaking your sales records. Creativity will put a huge "fun factor" into your job making selling more enjoyable, entertaining, and rewarding for both you and your customers. Once you have your imagination pump flowing, you'll fuel your efforts with high octane power that will put you on the sales superhighway!

"By logic and reason, we die hourly; by imagination we live."

—W. B. Yeats

Targeting
Your Creativity

Creativity can improve almost anything you do in selling and customer service. But it's easiest to begin with just one or two areas. Choose ones that reflect your personal priorities, tastes, and talents before liberating your imagination to engulf everything else. Here are a few activities to consider. Which ones do you want to start with?

- Getting more appointments faster with the "right people."
- Making your account management process more effective and efficient.
- Finding new uses for your product or service.
- Coming up with clever sales slogans.
- Improving time and territory management.
- Developing ideas to improve sales operations and administration.
- Using novel ways to smoothly close the "tough" sale.
- Writing more attention-getting and persuasive sales letters that get results.
- Improving the handling of tough objections and sales barriers.
- Making your sales presentations "sizzle."
- Coming up with more brilliant sales strategies that blast away your competitors.
- Giving more exciting product demonstrations.
- Closing your sales faster and easier.
- Improving your negotiating tactics.
- Getting more repeat customers and referrals.
- Writing eye-catching proposals that set you and your product/service apart from others.
- Finding powerful ways to deal with recurring or "unsolvable" customer problems.
- Getting more and better sales leads and qualified prospects.
- Identifying new product or service niches.

"Determine that the thing can and shall be done, and then we shall find the way."
—Abraham Lincoln

Amazing
Neuron City

Your brain—it's a simple lumpy-looking mass of gray matter weighing about three pounds. Yet it's the most complex object in the universe. Every second, over 100,000 different chemical reactions occur in your brain. And during creative activity, your neurons work even faster firing volleys of electrical stimulation that can suddenly erupt into an *aha!*—that wonderful Eureka! moment of insightful discovery.

Your brain soaks up almost a third of the energy consumed by your body. Its electrochemical process produces the equivalent of a 20 watt bulb! It's also a pharmaceutical laboratory manufacturing over 50 powerful psychoactive drugs such as endorphins, dopamine, and serotonin, which boost creativity. If your brain were on a street corner in a tough neighborhood, it would probably be busted for possession.

Scientists believe that your brain can accumulate information that would fill over 500 sets of encyclopedias. That's because it contains over 100 billion neuron cells, each as powerful as a computer. They are connected together in a staggering number of pathways estimated to be 10^{800} (that's right—ten followed by eight hundred zeroes!). A map of those pathways would probably take 27 years just to unfold.

Wouldn't it be nice if our brain came with detailed operating instructions? It's commonly believed that we use less than 1% of its capabilities. But experts admit they have no idea of the brain's ultimate potential. The ability, however, to produce ideas is infinite. We need to learn to tap into its wellspring of wonder. Developing creative thinking techniques is a start. What are you waiting for—use it or lose it. Fire up those neurons!

"If you can dream it, you can do it."
—Walt Disney

Use *Both* of Your Brains

The human brain is divided into a *right* and *left* cerebral hemisphere, connected by the *corpus collosum*, a thick nerve cable containing millions of fibers that transmits continuous information between these "two brains." We tend to develop a "dominant side" of our brain by favoring use of one side over the other. (It is said that politicians are the exception, because they use neither side of the brain, but compensate by speaking out of both sides of their mouths.)

The *left brain* is the practical, no-nonsense side that deals with structure, logic, reasoning, calculation, evaluation, analysis, organization, and problem solving. If you're task-oriented, precise, serious, pragmatic, "sensible," conventional, controlled, and objective, chances are you're *left-brained*. Engineers, scientists, accountants, lawyers, and people who slow down at yellow lights are often considered left-brained.

The *right brain* deals with imagination, fantasy, dreams, symbols, emotions, improvisation, intuition, and experimentation. If you love ideas, are nonconventional, subjective, nonverbal, risk-oriented, impulsive, and playful, you're probably *right-brained*. Artists, entertainers, designers, advertising people, inventors, and marketers/salespeople are typical examples of right-brained people.

A desirable goal is to be *whole-brained*—to develop and use *both* sides of your brain equally. Use your right brain for wild, imaginative ideas. Then, use your left brain to evaluate and bring them down to earth. If you work on strengthening the "weaker" side of your brain, you'll discover a dramatic increase in overall mental effectiveness.

"If your head is wax, don't walk in the sun."
—Ben Franklin

Who's Chicken to Think Right and Left?

Ask the *right brain* of salespeople why the chicken crossed the road and you might get a surprising answer—something like, "He was a country western singer on the way to croon a new ballad to his girlfriend, Chickadee, who was a waitress at the "Cock a Doodle Do" diner. While crossing the street, the chicken was abducted aboard a UFO where the aliens convinced him to form a new band with them called "Henpecked Hirbadites from Alpha Centuri."

The *left brain* of salespeople would tell you that the chicken crossed the road because the "Kernel" performed exhaustive demographic and market analysis. He confirmed that his new franchise, "Tennessee Lickin' Chicken," would be in an optimal traffic pattern location on the other side of the intersection 62.5 feet next to the diner.

Great ideas and solutions come from *combining* out-of-this-world *right*- and down-to-earth *left*-brain thinking. Always let your right brain take over *first*. Let your imagination freely roam into deep space to explore unusual possibilities in all directions (that's called "divergent" thinking). Dream, visualize, and tinker with wacky, wild, outrageous, and far-fetched ideas. Don't censor, limit, or analyze your ideas just yet.

After your imagination runs out of fuel, *then* let your left brain do its job to take your spaced-out ideas and bring them down to solid ground. Use it to evaluate and judge ideas. Eliminate those that are impractical and focus on (using, modifying, or enhancing) those that are best implementable (this is called "convergent" thinking). Getting your two brains to work together can solve that vexing riddle of why the chicken crossed the road!

"All great discoveries are made by men whose feelings run ahead of their thinking."

—C. H. Oarkhurst

Creativity Is
a Numbers Game

You've heard it before—selling is a numbers game. The more leads you find, the more prospects you evolve, and the more customers you develop. Creative idea generation is a numbers game too! The more ideas you come up with, the greater is your chance of hitting that big jackpot.

The process of coming up with ideas is called "ideation." The more you exercise your creative thinking, the more skilled you become at coming up with ideas. It's that simple. It's a fallacy that creative people have good ideas all the time. The opposite is true. Picasso created over 20,000 works of art, most of which were considered worthless. But he learned and sharpened his technique from each try.

Thomas Edison believed that it took hundreds and sometimes thousands of tries before you hit upon a blockbuster. And he felt that one must come up with ideas every day to keep the creative juices flowing. As one salesperson in our workshop put it, "I guess you've got to kiss a lot of frogs to find a prince." Pucker up!

Creative people know that they must develop the *habit* of coming up with lots of ideas. Even if you don't hit upon a mega-idea, all those small ideas add up—and put you way ahead of your competitors. Become an idea person who develops a love affair with ideas big or small. Who knows when you'll hit the jackpot that will take your selling to a level never before imagined. The odds are in your favor!

**"I think and think for months and years.
Ninety-nine times, the conclusion is false.
The hundredth time I am right."**

—Albert Einstein

As a Person Thinketh . . .

Peggy A. was a competent salesperson who longed to think of herself as being really creative. Then, a funny thing happened. Her friend Linda continually insisted that Peggy was very creative. She even provided examples. Peggy stopped doubting herself and started applying her imagination on a regular basis. Her sales exploded. Another case of the self-fulfilling prophecy in action: *what you think, you become!*

Too many of us don't envision ourselves as being "creative." Why? We think we need a high IQ or lots of education (preferably a Ph.D.). Or we think of a creative person as a "gifted artist"—a prodigy perhaps. These biases are false. Creativity isn't the birthright of a chosen few. Everyone is inherently creative. Simply tap in to your own reservoir of talent.

As the shoe ad says, "Just Do it!" Studies have shown that creativity training can quickly enable people to increase the quantity and quality of their ideas. Learn more about creative problem-solving and idea-generating techniques. Be creative in little ways every day. Becoming creative is like building any skill. The more you practice and stretch your imagination, the faster your ideas will come and the stronger they'll be.

Most important, feel good about your ideas. Don't pressure yourself to "perform" creatively on the job at all times. The common denominator of all creative people is that they feel they are creative and, as such, they *act the part*. Forget about seeing is believing. It's the reverse with creativity: believe in your own creativity and you'll see the results!

"Dream lofty dreams, and as you dream, so shall you become."

—James Allen

The Ultimate
"Can" Opener

"We *can't* win that account"; "I *can't* make my sales quota in that new territory"; "I *can't* get an appointment with him"; "I *can't* answer that objection." How often have you heard these complaints or mouthed them yourself? Don't you just want to smack these whiners and tell them to snap out of it? Well you can't do that (unless you want to get sued), but here's what you *can* do.

Recognize the power of a creative can-do attitude. As Jean Luc Picard, commander of the Starship *Enterprise,* says, "Things are only impossible until they're not." After all, the impossible is simply the untried. Believing that with creativity, "I'll find a way," helps you mentally to erase the "t" from "can't." It separates the "can" from "cannot." That's why creativity is the ultimate can opener.

Philip V., an insurance agent from Boston, tried to reach a major bank's CEO for over a year. Letters, phone calls, name dropping, sending gifts at holidays—*nothing* worked. The white flag of surrender was about to be hoisted until he used the "can" opener. He learned that the CEO was an avid football fan. Using the executive's photo from a banking magazine, he had his company's graphic designer go to work. She electronically "pasted" the CEO's face onto a photo of the body of his favorite team's quarterback. The photo was blown up lifesize, mounted on thick cardboard and delivered. Instead of holding a football, the CEO held a sign saying, "I'm going to tackle my retirement with the same gusto as my job!" This imaginative opener helped to later score a big sales touchdown!

> **"What lies behind us and what lies before us are tiny matters compared to what lies within us."**
> **—William Morrow**

Six-Step Creative Process

Creativity is a process, not just a behavior. Every creative idea should go through a *six-step* process. It can take seconds or years depending upon your mental makeup and the complexity of the idea. Here are the steps:

1. *Preparation.* You think about every aspect of your problem or idea, research it, and generally "brainload" (absorb information). You add the raw materials that will make up your idea.

2. *Incubation.* This is a waiting period where the "idea brew percolates." All the information you accumulated plus the desired outcome of your idea is stored in your subconscious. It works on it—figuring out an answer without you realizing that something is about to happen.

3. *Illumination.* This is when the light bulb comes on—the answer pops out suddenly seemingly out of nowhere. It's called the *Aha!* or *Eureka!* moment. You never know how, why, or when it will happen.

4. *Evaluation.* In this stage you judge every aspect of your idea and identify its pros and cons. You need to put your idea through a wringer—testing it and determining its application and value.

5. *Transformation.* Based upon the evaluation of your idea, you modify it and enhance it to make it more acceptable.

6. *Implementation.* Now you take your idea from imagination to reality. It becomes a new or improved product, service, process, system, or method. Your idea has arrived—congratulations!

"I do not seek, I find."
—Pablo Picasso

Brainload for Breakthroughs

The first step in the creative process is to "brainload"—fill your mind with as much *specific* information as you can about the problem, opportunity, or idea you're focusing on. You don't have to become an expert, but the more you research, read, and think about it, the greater is your probability of coming up with a superior solution. That's what famous scientist Louis Pasteur meant when he said, " . . . chance favors only the prepared mind."

Another strategy is to do *diverse brainloading*—by learning about and experiencing a wide range of seemingly unrelated topics and new situations. Creative breakthroughs involve putting together unlikely combinations—splicing ideas from disparate areas such as science, religion, philosophy, psychology, sports, architecture, entertainment, art, or ancient cultures. For example, one imaginative salesperson who studied classical warfare recycled concepts from some brilliant Macedonian military strategies such as those of Alexander the Great and successfully applied them against his surprised competitors.

Expand your mental horizons by becoming a well-rounded, eclectic book reader. And enjoy the diversity of topics in magazines and newspapers from *The Wall Street Journal* to *Cosmopolitan* to *National Geographic* to *Mad* magazine to *Architectural Digest* to *Scientific American* to, yes, even *The National Enquirer.* Go to comedy clubs, eat at unique restaurants, see more plays, and make friends from various cultures. When you experience more unique places, people, and situations, you'll find coming up with original and exciting ideas much easier. Shovel it in. Brainload!

"I didn't get my ideas from Mao, Lenin, or Ho. I got my ideas from the Lone Ranger."
—Jerry Rubin

Be Ready for the Sudden "Aha!"

Once you've started the thinking process by researching an idea or problem, your subconscious mind kicks in and begins working on an answer. Without your active participation, it tirelessly processes everything 7 days a week/24 hours a day even while you're asleep. Remember that the next time the boss catches you dozing off.

Creative people generally report that the *"Aha!"* or *"Eureka!"* moment, when an idea suddenly erupts seemingly out of nowhere, occurs at the least expected and often most peculiar times. Many say that it happens while they're taking a shower, preparing a meal, brushing their teeth, doing exercise, driving, getting dressed, watching TV, or even after making love.

Hundreds of ideas can pop into your mind during the week. These thoughts often have a half-life of minutes. Even clever ideas that you'd expect to easily recall can vanish (sometimes forever) unless recorded immediately. Remember your mother's advice never to leave home without clean underwear because you might get in an accident? We say never leave home without clean notepads because you might get an idea.

Keep a notepad and pen with you at all times, even by your bedside. Or dictate your ideas into a microcassette recorder and transcribe them on a frequent basis. With a laptop computer or personal digital assistant, you can record and organize your ideas effectively. One ardent creative soul even has a waterproof pad and crayon in his shower so as not to miss that grand elusive *"Aha!"* moment. Of course, many people say his ideas are all wet.

"The intellect has little to do on the road to discovery. There comes a leap in consciousness, call it intuition or what you will, and the solution comes to you and you don't know how or why."

—Albert Einstein

Evaluating Your Idea or Solution

Once you've developed your idea or solution, put it to a "scrutiny test" to see how feasible and worthy of widespread acceptance it might be. This testing phase can help you identify weaknesses and flaws in your idea or solution so you can correct them before you propose your idea to others. Following is a checklist to help you.

☐ Is my idea simple to grasp and "obvious," or is it too clever, complex, or ingenious?

☐ What are all the possible pros and cons of my idea?

☐ Who will benefit most and least from the idea?

☐ Who should I ask to give me effective feedback and advice on enhancing the idea?

☐ Should I develop several variations of the idea or solution to let people more easily choose one over the others?

☐ What are all the possible uses/applications of the idea? Can parts of the idea be used elsewhere?

☐ How would I react if my idea was proposed by others (boss, competitors, etc.)?

☐ Whose support and commitment are critical in getting my idea accepted and implemented? What is my strategy personally to enlist the support of each person?

☐ Has my idea been tried before? What were the results and why? Why is my idea different and superior? Why do I feel/know it will be successful now?

☐ What are all the obstacles I might face in getting it accepted and implemented? What is my persuasive strategy to counter obstacles?

☐ What resources do I need to get the idea or opportunity implemented?

☐ Is the timing right or is it ahead of its time? If it is "too visionary," what should I do?

"People will accept your idea much more readily if you tell them Benjamin Franklin said it first."

—David H. Comins

Cleaning the Windows of Opportunity

Entrepreneurial salespeople think about ways to act quickly to exploit fully the opportunities that others might overlook or ignore. They're constantly on the alert to spot and think about *when* and *how* to use something to their advantage. Like alchemy turning lead into gold, creative thinking can almost magically transmute someone's problems, needs, or goals into lucrative sales and service opportunities for you.

Creative salespeople read and network a lot. Why? So they can spot new or evolving trends, developments, and fads. These generate opportunities for any product or service. Smart *opportunity exploiters* pounce on a good situation before the window of opportunity slams shut. There's nothing more painful than getting your fingers caught in the window of opportunity.

Creative people are always looking for answers to questions such as the following:

> "How can I use this new technology to help me or my sales team in some way?"

> "With the change in the economy, how can I creatively help my customers more now?"

> "How can I get off to a great start with my new sales manager?"

> "How can I use this problem to my advantage?"

> "I wonder how I might work together with this new president of the Chamber of Commerce to get extra sales contacts?"

> "How can I imaginatively use this interesting advertising slogan I just heard to make a major point with my customers?"

> "How can I apply what I've seen at this trade show to help me get a competitive edge?"

"The people who get on in this world are the people who get up and look for the circumstances they want, and, if they can't find them, make them."

—George Bernard Shaw

Get Wild
and Crazy

Whether you call them breakthroughs, quantum leaps, paradigm shifts, discovery jumps, or superinnovations, they are caused by radically different ideas put forth by gutsy, imaginative people. You can develop "practical and sensible" ideas of modest value or you can take the straightjacket off your imagination to let it soar heaven-bound by playing around with wacky, shocking, ridiculous, weird, bizarre, and outrageous ideas that will lead to mind-boggling improvements. Post no limits to your thoughts!

Bold and daring approaches must be permitted and explored if you want to make the most out of creativity. Permitting yourself to be impractical, illogical, and even silly gives a powerful jolt to unlock your thinking into the doorway of the infinite. Besides . . . it's great fun! People can "piggyback," "leapfrog," and "springboard" off each other's unusual ideas and develop more practical offshoots of them later. Or, they could extract some valuable, more usable elements from each of the wild ideas and combine them to form a real megaton hit.

During one "anything goes" sales department creativity session for a large Chicago printing company, the goal was to find ways to keep more repeat customers. One person suggested that "they arrest their customers and lock them up." Her colleague picked up on it and said, "What if we just fined them for scooting to a competitor," while another salesperson reversed that idea and said, "How about giving them incentives to stick with us." They came up with a clever and attractive incentive program that "locked" customers in.

"The reasonable man adapts himself to the world; the unreasonable one persists in trying to adapt the world to himself. Therefore all progress depends on the unreasonable man."

—George Bernard Shaw

Think "Outside the Box"

A simple way to understand creativity is to assume that thinking occurs in a kind of box. When you keep an open mind, you expand your box. When you limit yourself with lots of rules, regulations, formulas, and set ways of doing things, you shrink your box and clutter it up. So you're less able to exercise your imagination by mentally moving around. You keep tripping over old habits and preconceptions.

A lesson from a Zen master demonstrates the importance of "cleaning out" your thinking box. The Zen master invited a student for tea. When he arrived, the Zen master poured tea into the student's cup. The master continued pouring even as the tea overflowed and spilled onto the table and floor. "Master," the student cried, "you must stop now. The tea is overflowing and not going into my cup." The sage replied, "The same is true with you, my bright son. You must first empty what you have in your mind's cup if you are to effectively receive my teaching and ideas."

What can we learn from the Zen master? Three things. First, your mind can overflow with information and knowledge. Second, you must toss out your biases, outdated information, and preconceptions to make way for radically new breakthrough ideas. Three, don't wear a new suit when you're having tea with a Zen master.

And four, "think outside the box" as often and as much as possible. This will break the boundaries of tradition and vault you into the uncluttered infinite space of innovation. That's where you'll discover galactic-size fresh approaches and solutions. Next time someone tells *you* to take a flying leap, do it mentally—leap outside the box.

"You have no right to erect your toll-gate upon the highways of thought."
—Robert G. Ingersoll

In Case of
Emergency . . .
Think

Doug H. and his family operated a successful auto brake and transmission repair business for 15 years in a midsize western town. When a franchise opened up right across from them, it sported a bright sign, "$89.95 Brake Job." That undercut their price by $20. "How can I compete with a franchise that can buy their parts, machines, and tools at better discounts than I can and train their mechanics less expensively?" Doug bellowed.

Doug felt depressed. He figured he only had two losing options: keep his price to make a profit, in which case he'd lose business *fast*, or lower his price to compete and go out of business *slowly*. "Not much of a choice," he lamented. "What will I do now?" He feared he was cornered in a business cul-de-sac. His knew his mechanics were top-notch and they tried always to totally satisfy his customers.

He was close to throwing in the towel, but his wonderfully supportive wife, Kathie, kept encouraging him to get out of his mental rut and begin thinking out of the box. "How can I not lose sales and *still* keep my price to survive?" he asked his subconscious mind. "What other imaginative strategies can I use to get people to see past just a lower price?" he pondered. Growing confident that a creative solution was somehow possible, he kept trying to think outside the box. A week later, a huge sign was placed high atop his building with big bold letters: **"Our Experts Fix $89.95 Brake Jobs!"** He and Kathie also came up with 16 other neat ideas that would help differentiate his service from the competition's. Creative thinking and a great wife were his lucky breaks (pun intended)!

"The trouble with most people is that they think with their hopes or fears or wishes rather than with their minds."

—Will Durant

Are *You* a Risk-Taker?

"Taking risks" is very relative term (especially if you take risks lending money to your relatives). *Risk-avoiders* dread any risk (however slight) and always want to "play it safe." *Risk-takers* take occasional chances when it seems fairly likely they will gain from it. *Risk-thrivers* live on the adrenaline edge by aggressively seeking all-or-nothing situations that offer significant payoffs if not spectacular losses. Where do *you* fit within these three categories?

You have a propensity for risk if you:

- ✹ Seek "thrills" on a regular basis.
- ✹ Work strictly on sales commissions.
- ✹ Speed up at yellow lights.
- ✹ Tell Frank Sinatra to do it your way.
- ✹ Have a habit of breaking rules.
- ✹ Voice your opinion even if it's unpopular.
- ✹ Are not afraid of rejection from others.
- ✹ Have been told by friends that you take more chances than most people.
- ✹ Go bungee jumping with a plain rope.
- ✹ Have a personal philosophy that you only live once, so why not *live it!*
- ✹ Seldom listen to the solemn overblown cautions of others.
- ✹ Go on a roller coaster after downing four hot dogs and six beers.
- ✹ Buy insurance from a guy named Pee Wee.
- ✹ Own your own business or mind somebody else's.
- ✹ Go camping without toilet paper.

Taking calculated risks is an important part of being creative. Not taking any risk can be risky. Don't be addicted to caution!

"Behold the turtle: He only makes progress when he sticks his neck out."
                                    —James Bryant Conant

Paradigm Shifting Into High Gear

Paradigms are mental models or patterns of our world. They are accepted ways of thinking or doing things that guide people in their work and daily lives. "Shifting" or "breaking a paradigm" means going from conventional to *un*conventional wisdom. This can produce exciting new discoveries, courses of action or direction, and quantum leap innovations.

When Columbus discovered America, he broke the paradigm that the world was flat. Sixteenth-century astronomer Copernicus shattered the paradigm that the earth was the center of the solar system by proving that the sun was the center. Treating customers respectfully and cordially is a paradigm shift for some salespeople. Paradigms, whether they're sales philosophies, practices, values, or ideas, dig into our subconscious, making change a drawn-out and tough process.

How many sales practices and concepts do you still employ long after their usefulness and validity have expired? Are you still selling in a flat world? Think about how you might create a breakthrough paradigm shift in your sales or service operations. Envision the possible implications of the new paradigm. For example, instead of persuading people to buy, how would your selling change if you primarily focused on educating them or entertaining them? What would happen if you somehow cooperated with select competitors instead of treating them as deadly adversaries? How might "cyberselling" over the information superhighway radically transform operations? Using imaginative thinking to create a paradigm shift can propel your selling into a new galaxy of opportunity—at warp speed!

"A long habit of not thinking a thing wrong gives it a superficial appearance of being right."

—Thomas Paine

A Car Dealer Who "$hifted" $elling

Ned F. owned ten automobile dealerships on the East Coast. He had a vivid dream one evening that customers were "partying" in his stores. *Vroom!* His paradigm suddenly shifted to overdrive: Make car buying *enjoyable* and *fun*. He asked his eighty-three salespeople for ideas to create a playful and out-of-the ordinary buying climate. Here's a sample of some of the twenty-nine ideas implemented:

> ✱ An old-fashioned popcorn cart (with that wonderful aroma) was put in each location.
> ✱ A "game room" was created. Video games, pinball machines, and nonelectronic games occupied children while their parents shopped.
> ✱ Big blow-up pictures (with funny buying captions under them) of old-time comedians such as Abbott & Costello, Lucille Ball, Redd Foxx, and others were placed around the showroom for a relaxed and amusing effect.
> ✱ "Movies" were made starring customers. When they picked up their vehicles, their salesperson videotaped them performing lines from cue cards as they entered their car, pulled off the lot, etc. The video footage was then fed into a multimedia computer program designed to edit the customer's performance quickly, easily, and inexpensively into pre-existing scenes. Customers could choose to star in a race (with their sports car), a cowboy truck rodeo (using their truck), or two other more sedate sedan/luxury car scenes. The edited version showed the new owner and vehicle playing a role with other actors in a 5-minute movie.

Thrilled "star treatment" customers couldn't wait to show their videotape to *everyone*. That clever publicity "produced and directed" many referral sales.

"No idea is so outlandish that it should not be considered with a searching but at the same time with a steady eye."
                                                    —Winston Churchill

Innovation:
Imagination With
Action

Creativity is about coming up with ideas. *Innovation* is about implementing them. Innovation is a structured method of taking flashes of genius to develop them into new or improved products, services, processes, manufacturing techniques, or other commercial ventures. It begins with a great idea and ends in the marketplace. Creativity is about *thinking;* innovation is about *doing.*

Sales innovation involves putting to work new ways to sell and service, improving administrative procedures, or any other advancements in overall sales operations and planning. Whether it's using new technology or simply redesigning the way things are done, smart sales organizations *continuously improve everything they do.* They make innovation a timeless "routine." To boost innovation, *sales managers should:*

✱ Assess their organization culture to identify what beliefs, values, and norms need to be changed to speed up innovation.
✱ Prioritize opportunities to apply innovation.
✱ Design a strategy to make innovation a top objective of the organization.
✱ Identify and get resources for innovation.
✱ Design a system or process to ensure that bold new ideas get implemented in a predictable and efficient way.
✱ Enlist the support of influential people to champion the cause of innovation.
✱ Tell sales and service staff they're fired if they don't come up with some brilliant new ideas pronto (just kidding!).

Because innovation is about acting upon imagination, it's been called *imaginaction.* Imagine that!

"Ideas won't keep. Something must be done with them."

—Alfred North

Sales Innovation
Is
"Applied Failure"

Let's talk about the "F" word—*failure*. It's the castor oil of success! It may not be fun going down, but the result makes up for it. *Innovation is all about failing and making mistakes.* Unless you develop a tolerant—even optimistic—attitude toward setbacks, you'll never be able to get your ideas into high gear. The more failures you allow yourself, the greater your chance for success.

Condition yourself for trial-and-error mistakes. They act as lightposts illuminating the way to solutions. Remember: your goal is to *fail forward*—always learning something that will get you closer to where you're aiming. There's no such thing as an uneventful, straight line toward implementing a great idea. Innovating means trying something new, untried, untested. It involves blind alleys and confusion. Expect to stumble and trip as you explore the darkness and the unknown. It's the only way to learn what works and what doesn't. Cabdrivers do it all the time—especially in New York.

Does failure bruise the ego and self-esteem? Only if you let it. Inoculate yourself against failure by realizing that it's an inherent part of creativity. Be patient with yourself. Hang in there. Give yourself credit when you made an intelligent effort that didn't work. The only real mistake you can make is giving up too soon. Just ask the person who invented Preparation G. If you haven't failed a lot, you haven't tried enough. Weathering the setbacks is what separates the *innovators* from the *imitators!*

"No great deed is done by falterers who ask for certainty."

—George Eliot

Devil's Advocate . . . Must You?

One sales executive half-jokingly told us, "The best way to kill an idea around here is to take it to a meeting." It's unfortunate, but true. It's a natural human instinct to immediately judge ideas. People want to play "devil's advocate." They want to strafe you with a list of reasons why an idea *won't* work. What's the result of this premature and rash evaluation? Many great ideas end up on the trash heap of what might have been. The putdowns to squelch an idea are as numerous as the meetings in which they occur. Any of these sound familiar?

"We tried that before and it didn't work."

"That idea will never fly around here."

"Too impractical . . . too risky."

"I just don't like it—it doesn't grab me"

"We shouldn't consider it for two (three, four, five, etc.) reasons."

Some folks actually feel they are doing everyone a favor by playing devil's advocate. They think it saves discussion time. It doesn't. Worse yet, *you* may be the one listening to your devilish inner voice. Don't let it strangle your own fledgling ideas waiting to soar. Instead of focusing on an idea's weakness, focus on its positive aspects and strengths. List all the reasons why the idea might work. Condition yourself to first think optimistically about an idea. Even if the idea turns out to be lousy, it's amazing how many good ideas it might eventually lead to. The next time someone badgers you with, "Let me play devil's advocate . . ." tell him or her, "Hey . . . how about playing *angel's* advocate?" And do the same with your inner voice.

"New ideas are not born in a conforming environment."

—Roger Von Oech

Rubbing In by Rubbing Off

Pamela G. is part of a group of six creative customer support reps for an appliance manufacturer who meet monthly to develop novel ideas for solving problems gnawing away at their support operations. They call themselves "The Createers." And they all love bouncing ideas off each other. Each feels highly energized by the collective excitement generated within the group. Each feels free to push his or her imagination to its limits. "Ideas are rubbing in as we're rubbing off on each other," one said.

To *amplify* your creativity, hang out with other creative people who "play off" each other and support free-wheeling, off-the-wall imaginative ideas while suspending premature judgment. Feel the power of minds expanding and melding—reaching toward new breakthroughs. Get together with people who want to have fun being creative and who want to make a real difference at the same time. Make friends of diverse creative personalities in the arts, sciences, entertainment, and in other fields. Their imaginative energy, love of life, optimism, novel perspectives on things, and deep-seated belief in the need to be creative will rub off on you and uplift you to new heights of creative thinking and action.

Avoid "energy vampires"—those negative, self-defeating types who fear the daylight of new ideas and the fresh air of change. Who suck the fledgling thoughts and creative force from deep within you. Something "magical" happens when you're around people who thrive on being creative. Something very *useful* happens too!

> **"The creative act thrives in an environment of mutual stimulation, feedback, and constructive criticism—all in a community of creativity."**
>
> **—William T. Brady**

Kiss Your Big "But" Good-Bye

Glenda S. and Charles C. had the biggest "buts" in their Baltimore commercial real estate office. And they'd push their big "buts" in the way of anyone who wanted to try out new sales and service ideas. Here are some examples:

"I'd like to do it, *but* I don't have the time."

"That's a clever idea, *but* we'll never get people to cooperate on it."

"I'd like to sell more in that territory, *but* our competitors have it locked up tight."

"We ought to change the way we operate, *but* not now."

"I'd like to be more creative in selling, *but* it's too bothersome and risky."

Their fat "buts" blocked the view of the window of opportunity. Anytime their managers or customers asked them to do anything new, different, or even slightly out of the ordinary, they'd stick their big "buts" in everyone's faces. The word "but" is extremely dangerous. It pierces the (oftentimes thin) armor of optimism and motivation. It provides an excuse for inaction and procrastination. It rationalizes defeat before the battle even begins. Worse yet, like a catching affliction, it can spread to others quickly. Whole organizations can come down with chronic "but-itis."

One day their sales manager, Claire J., just couldn't take it anymore. "I've had it with all this impossibility thinking around here," she bellowed at Glenda and Charles, who reeled back in surprise. "It's about time I kicked some 'buts' around here." And she did. She started a "Just say yes" campaign. Work together with others in your sales group to get rid of stale weak excuses. Sayonara—kiss your "buts" good-bye!

> **"Loser: someone who complains about the noise when opportunity is knocking hard."**
>
> **—Anonymous**

Super Duper Rejection Protection

The bigger, more radical, more visionary, more daring your idea, the more skepticism and resistance it will receive. Don't expect any idea, no matter how brilliant, to be quickly accepted, let alone embraced. *Ideas have to be sold.* The key is perseverance and a diehard determination to never give up—to keep eventual victory in sight.

Every person of visionary genius has been told that they would not succeed, that their ideas were crazy or useless. Chester Carlson knew that all too well. He swore he had discovered something of mega-importance. But his creation was initially greeted with resounding indifference. Critics said his invention was "interesting," but it had no future and no real application. Undaunted, Carlson refused to believe them. Instead, he drew strength from his faith in himself and his idea.

After more than two decades of mountainous disappointment, exhaustion, and rejection, Carlson's remarkable determination paid off. His invention took off. It was wildly successful. And Carlson earned hundreds of millions of dollars, much of which he gave away to charity. Today it's hard to believe that anyone could have rejected Carlson's invention for more than 20 years. You know it as the Xerox machine.

Management guru Peter Drucker says that no breakthrough occurs without the involvement of a "monomaniac with a mission." Don't listen to the nay-sayers. Remember: Earth-shaking ideas appear meager when passed through the sieve of small, petty minds! A lot of people have great ideas. Few invest in the stamina to see them through. With enough time, energy, patience, and stick-to-itness, you *can't* fail.

"You are never quite at ease about a new idea born in your mind, for you do not know in what storms of contradiction it may involve you."

—Jean Guiber

Disconnect
Your Autopilot

Most people behave without paying attention. We eat, drive, talk, work, think, and generally act in set patterns acquired over a lifetime. *They're called habits.* Although some add order and predictability to our lives, many are staunch enemies of creativity. As we continually repeat behaviors, we cease to be conscious of them. We go on "autopilot"—mindlessly and robotically "doing what we've always done and getting what we've always gotten," as one bumper sticker philosopher said.

When we're on autopilot, we accept things at face value. We don't wonder if there's a better way of doing things. Whether it's writing sales letters, answering phones, doing paperwork, or planning our day, we just keep on keeping on. Unaware of our mindless state, we're not open to fresh perspectives and new information. Habits can be so powerful and comfortable that people refuse to shed them even when a behavior has become ineffective or *counterproductive!* But it can be done, and it must be if you want to develop breakthrough sales and service ideas.

Carol F., a sales executive of an office machines manufacturer, had her staff critically reexamine *every* aspect of their sales and service operations: methods, rules, policies, administrative procedures, assumptions, and planning techniques. At a two-day meeting, her goal was to have her staff self-discover all those outdated ideas and work habits that people were blindly obedient to. She then had them apply creative thinking to "reengineer" their operations. However, she proposed a new "habit" to stick to: *continuous innovation!*

"Habit, if not resisted, soon becomes necessity."

—St. Augustine

Being in a
Mental Rut

How often do you feel as though you're in a mental rut at your job or in your life? That's a condition we call "trench brain." You're stuck in a negative thinking and dead feeling black hole that's sucking you deeper and deeper into an abyss of apathy or despair. Does any of the following describe your mental attitude or the general mood of others at your office?

* ❀ Your mantra is "Who cares?"
* ❀ You feel like going down the drain even though you've stopped showering.
* ❀ You don't laugh when you imagine your boss unexpectedly getting caught in traffic after taking a strong laxative.
* ❀ You're waiting to win the lottery, but you haven't purchased a ticket.
* ❀ Your (still-visiting) in-laws don't bother you any longer.
* ❀ You believe there's a vacuum in outer space because life on earth sucks.
* ❀ You take an inkblot test and everything looks like Dr. Rorschach or his pets.
* ❀ You go through the day with a glazed look and no remembrance of what happened.
* ❀ You very eagerly await going to lunch at 8 A.M.
* ❀ You're thinking of vacationing in Russia.
* ❀ You believe that showing up doesn't matter; showing off is 90% of the job.
* ❀ You can't touch your finger to your nose even before you get drunk.

Creativity is not a cure-all. But once it's practiced in your sales organization, it's less likely that people will be afflicted with "trench brain." Help yourself and others to stay out of their mental rut!

"If you haven't changed your mind lately, are you sure that you have one?"

—Bumper sticker

Computers + Creativity = Awe$ome

The "digital revolution" has begun. With today's exciting computers, software programs, color printers, scanners, and clipart/media, you can create compelling proposals, letters, brochures, and other sales support materials. Salespeople who exploit the enormous potential of computer power will leave their competitors in the dust.

Why write a dull text-only sales letter when you can add color, photos, pictures, and graphics. Brainstorm ways to use desktop publishing to customize such materials as color banners, newsletters, invitations, announcements, or agendas quickly and inexpensively. Give flair to your style—stand out from the crowd!

Computerized *multimedia* with its text, graphics, video, animation, and CD-quality sound will persuasively hold your customers spellbound. Your sales department can create stunning "drop-dead impressive" multimedia sales presentations that dramatically showcase your products and services. Joe D., a sales executive with a Fortune 500 computer workstation manufacturer, firmly believes in this high-tech sales approach. He often incorporates film and video clips into his sales presentations to get a laugh and make a point. A *Saturday Night Live* sketch about building a car proved highly effective as part of a pitch to Detroit automakers. And Joe D. loves to make points about teamwork with scenes of gangsters working together in *The Untouchables*. Why does he do it? He can't afford not to. "We live in a TV and sound bite-oriented culture," he explains. "You need to be creative to get impact." Use computer muscle to make your ideas soar.

"I do not fear computers. I fear the lack of them."

—Isaac Asimov

"Techno-Smart" Way to Grab Attention

Mary W., an account manager for a major consulting firm, wanted to land a new account by pitching her firm's "reengineering process." She telephoned the account's chief operating officer, who asked that she send descriptive literature of the consulting/training program.

Her intuition told her that if she mailed brochures, he would not take the time to understand the program's real value and impact. "Was there a better, *more clever* way to give that information such that it would motivate him to meet with me?" she asked herself. Two days later, a blockbuster idea erupted from her subconscious: write a personalized "success story" about the executive and his company *as if* they had already implemented the reengineering program from her firm (postdated nine months in the future).

Using her computer's desktop publishing program, Mary designed and wrote a "fictitious" (but real-looking) two-page industry-type newsletter. Her attention-grabbing headline read: *(Customer's) Co. Reengineers With Significant Results!* On the top left of the front page was a picture of the chief operating officer (she scanned his picture in from their annual report) with a caption underneath, *Mr. (name) was the key architect of the successful process.* The concise "article" specifically and persuasively told how the reengineering process worked and focused on the impressive operational and financial benefits that would have resulted. This customized imaginative touch landed her the sale. Since then, Mary has discovered over a dozen other ingenious ways to use her computer to "take the byte" out of sales problems and brilliantly outshine her competitors every time.

"If an idea cannot be expressed in terms of people, it is a sure sign it is irrelevant to the real problems of life."

—Colin Wilson

Wake Up
the Sleeping Artist
in You

To tap deeper into your (right brain) creative and intuitive nature, consider taking up creative activities or adding to those in which you're already involved. You can release new sources of pent-up imagination and build your idea-generating self-confidence by just beginning to do more "creative stuff." Resourceful solutions to business and personal problems can be stimulated through new thinking modes brought on by developing your latent artistic side.

Through expressing yourself more in one way, you'll expand your thinking powers in other directions as well. Unfortunately, too many people doggedly refuse to admit any tendency toward artistic creation. They think that one must be exceptionally gifted or prone to creative "talent" before one even attempts to begin. Everyone has some artistic side waiting to spring forth if summoned. You don't have to be especially accomplished at that activity to benefit from it. Simply exercising your artistic right brain will strengthen its powers. Even hobbies can act as creativity builders. Think about what you'd like to do and then just try it without worrying about mastering it right away. Here are some things to consider:

- ✸ gourmet cooking
- ✸ painting
- ✸ model building
- ✸ dancing
- ✸ drawing
- ✸ comedy
- ✸ public speaking
- ✸ decorating
- ✸ arts and crafts
- ✸ woodworking
- ✸ crochet and needlework
- ✸ singing
- ✸ acting
- ✸ graphic arts
- ✸ home entertaining
- ✸ writing

"A first-rate soup is more creative than a second-rate painting."

—Abraham Maslow

Exercise to Get in a Thinking Mood

Exercise is a great way to start ideas flowing. Physical exercise boosts endorphins and oxygen in your brain, relaxing you and helping to prime your imagination pump. Exercise drains stress and provides an overall feeling of wellness and confidence, which facilitates creative thinking.

Unfortunately, many people do the wrong exercises. They fly off the handle, jump to conclusions, step on toes, push their luck, carry things too far, run down others' opinions, throw their weight around, dodge responsibility, and toss good ideas away prematurely. These actions may be great if you're a member of Congress, but they're inappropriate for solving problems or generating ideas. Effective exercises remove your conscious mind from working on a problem or idea and allow your *sub*conscious mind to bring it more effectively to the surface.

The best physical exercises to boost thinking are those that are not so competitive and vigorous that they use all your energy and concentration. Mild-to-moderate exercise that is enjoyable works best. Here are some:

* ❀ Relaxed walks alone or with friends.
* ❀ Running, bicycling, swimming, rowing.
* ❀ Hiking along a scenic path.
* ❀ Shooting hoops.
* ❀ Making love; giving or getting a massage.
* ❀ Aerobic routines.
* ❀ Yoga.

Maintain a regular program of exercise. It'll keep your mental conditioning fit and sharp.

"Inability to relax, to let go of a problem, often prevents its solution."
—Eugene Raudsepp

Create an Inspiring Shangri-La

The "right" work environment will stir up your creative juices. An office space that makes you feel free, relaxed, comfortable, motivated, energized, inspired, optimistic, and powerful will help keep you in a creative mood. Of course, not all of us can have a fancy office in Congress. So you need to design your own creative think-oasis.

Determine the "climate" you want to breed and foster. What visual and audio stimuli will make you feel good? Decorate your work space with art objects (statues, pictures, sculptures), plants, posters/signs, novelty items, pictures of loved ones, stuffed animals, "goofy stuff" (that makes you smile), awards, memorabilia, and fun collectibles. Put in a fish tank, neon signs, and toys. Add more color. Be creative. *Be you!*

Decorate with comfortable furniture that invites others to come in and discuss ideas with you. Use soft, indirect lighting (tracks, small lamps, and dimmers) to enhance a positive mood and relieve stress. Select music that drains away tension and helps peak your mental alertness. Many creative people prefer classical music, but listen to what tickles your imagination.

These suggestions may sound hokey, but we've included them because we know that *they work!* Thomas T., an electronic components sales executive from a northeastern company, has an interesting office that features a real (refurbished) slot machine for people to "play with." It symbolizes that coming up with ideas requires a lot of tries to hit a jackpot. We think he's hit one.

"Each of us makes his own weather, determines the color of the skies in the emotional universe which he inhabits."
—Bishop Fulton J. Sheen

Play at Work and Have Fun!

We bet there's a direct correlation between more mirth, merriment, and joking at work and decreased staff usage of stuff like Excedrin, Maalox, Valium, and Advil. Unfortunately, not enough managers understand the importance and real value of encouraging *proper* fun and play in the workplace. A fun workplace stimulates creative juices, boosts cooperation and teamwork, increases productivity, and prevents burnout.

A stern, solemn, boring, or rigid work climate breeds apathy, anxiety, or bland conformity. "Fun" at work is any activity that enhances the psychological well-being of people and invigorates them to be alert, thought-filled, and productive. Fun is fun. Of course, stupid, unsafe, immature, or personally hurtful stunts are just plain dumb. We're endorsing situations and a work environment that enable people to let their hair down, be themselves, have some laughs, and just loosen up a bit. Here are some ideas:

- ⊛ Show videos of cartoons or old comedy movies during meetings or at lunch.
- ⊛ Have regular popcorn parties.
- ⊛ Give out humorous work awards.
- ⊛ Pass out sponge balls at meetings. Throw them at people who try to squelch ideas prematurely.
- ⊛ Play games that build teamwork.
- ⊛ Perform humorous skits during holidays (see more examples in the back of the book).

The right type of "nonsense" makes sense. Get yourself and others to live the saying, "When I play, I play and when I work, I *play!*"

"Play so that you may be serious."
—Anarcharsis, 600 B.C.

The Humor and Creativity Connection

Humor can do more than bust up a creative block. It can super-
charge overall creativity at all times. Have you ever noticed how
much you laugh during a good brainstorming session? There's
a reason for this phenomenon—humor and creativity are inextricably linked. Just ask Alice M. Isen. As a University of Mary-
land psychology professor, she found that people are more creative when they're in a good mood. According to *American Health*
magazine, Isen's studies revealed that happy people are more
creative in word association, categorization, and memory tasks.
She explained her findings: "Someone who is happy can perceive
subtle relationships between things because positive material is
stimulated in his memory. He has more ideas."

A practical application of Isen's research was reported in
US Air magazine. A consultant advised a company to forgo coats
and ties during creativity meetings. In response, the company
purchased a number of Hawaiian shirts. Despite complaints
about the new garb, the president insisted that the shirts be worn
during the meetings. He noticed positive results—people light-
ened up just by donning the shirts. By the time a meeting started,
they were "relaxed and ready to roll." A playful frame of mind
and environment is very conducive to creativity. As Dr. Stu Silverstein notes, "Humor can put you in a relaxed state—not Ore-
gon, but close." Go ahead—how about wearing a colorful
lampshade to match the Hawaiian shirt? Get rid of your imagination cobwebs with some good laughs. You'll quickly see ha ha
ha ha turn to *Aha!*

> **"Your brain is too tense—too tenths the
> size of a normal brain."**
>   **—Abbott and Costello**

Fake It or Make It . . . Laugh Either Way

With creativity as with sales, you're either psyched up or psyched out. Some days everything is clicking and the world is a beautiful place. It's like standing in an open field during a brainstorm—you're being showered with ideas. Other days you're so unimaginative, you couldn't even dream the *possible* dream.

So what do you do when you're out of flash? Laugh as loud, long, and as often as you wish (but do it alone in a soundproof room). Scientists tell us that even faking laughter—forcing it until it becomes natural—provides benefits. Laughter is physical exercise that combats the sluggishness you feel from a creative block. A good belly laugh raises your body temperature, increases blood pressure, activates endorphins in your brain, and alleviates tension. This reinvigorates your thought engine of ingenuity.

Dr. William Fry, professor emeritus of psychiatry at Stanford University, said that laughing 100 times a day is the exercise equivalent of 10 minutes of rowing! (Of course, 10 minutes of rowing can lead to 100 laughs—it just depends on who's rowing.) Laughter has been called "internal jogging. " It keeps the imagination muscles toned.

Picasso said, "Every child is an artist. The problem is how to remain an artist after he grows up." Children actually laugh an average of about 400 times a day, whereas adults laugh only 15 times. Maybe as we grow older we need just to keep laughing. Studying his patients, Freud believed, "Laughter is a means of unconscious sexual release." If true, that makes a person sexy as well as creative and fun to be around. Are you at least smiling yet?

"Man's most serious activity is play."
—George Santayana

"Funny Business" With Your Customers

Creative humor can work absolute wonders for your sales and customer service organization to speed you miles ahead of your competitors. Hungry for some food for thought? Next time you're in Greenville, Maine, stop by the Roadkill Cafe, a top tourist attraction. They'll serve you up a sense of humor you'll never forget. Two favorites on their menu are the "Bye-Bye Bambi Burger" and the "Chicken That Didn't Make It Across The Road" sandwich.

And it's not just the food names that are funny. It's the preparation. According to a 1993 Associated Press story by Michelle Kearns, one cook often yells, "down boy, down boy" while preparing chicken breasts for the grill. He sometimes throws feathers in the dining area. No, the Roadkill is not your average cafe! Did you hear a horn that sounds like a goose or moose? Or maybe it was a loud cowbell. Don't worry. It's just the kitchen staff signaling that an order is ready. Every server responds to a different noise. And customers respond too. They think it's hysterical.

Co-owners Mariette Sinclair and Leigh Turner make a major effort to encourage humorous creativity. Here's how Turner explained it to the Associated Press: "What we tell servers who come to work for us is you may do anything you like in service of your guests qualified by only two restrictions—you can't offend anybody and we want to hear laughter coming out of your tables." It works. What kind of "funny business" can you add when selling and servicing your customers?

"Life is too serious to be taken seriously."
—Oscar Wilde

What an Excuse!

Nobody's perfect (all right, present company excluded). No matter how much quality customer service you promote, mistakes will occur. What separates top sales performers from the pack is *how* the mistakes are handled. Let's look at a common mistake—speeding. Ever try to talk your way out of a speeding ticket? Many try, few succeed. In fact, the Georgia Fraternal Order of Police has held a contest for the wildest excuses offered. In 1984, a top winner was Sheriff's Deputy Daniel Fogarty. According to the *San Jose Mercury News,* Fogarty told of "an overweight driver who had developed a 'fear factor' method of losing weight. The man told Fogarty that the faster he drove, the more afraid he became of being caught and therefore the more calories he burned off.

Fogarty said fatty's creativity was so impressive that no ticket was written" (emphasis added). Some sales job!

When a customer catches you in an error, do you make excuses or do you make *Excuses!*—outlandish and amusing whoppers that are so creative and entertaining, they charm and disarm customers transforming their attitude from negative to positive. Obviously you need to gauge your customer's personality and avoid the cute and funny stuff if there is a serious mistake that needs no-nonsense, kid-glove handling. But for those other situations, why not flex your imagination and get a laugh by telling your customer her shipment was delayed because your service manager was bitten by a rabid werewolf. But he promises a "howling success" with customer shipments from now on!

**"Many things are not believed because
their current explanation is not believed."
—Friedrich Nietzsche**

Heating Up Cold
Calls With Humor

Wayne S., a professional telemarketer, was stymied in his attempts to reach an executive because the bigshot's secretary
wouldn't put Wayne's calls through. Although this problem is
common, Wayne's approach was unique. He asked the secretary,
"What's your name?" She said, "I'm his secretary." He queried,
"Is that what you go by?" She replied, Well . . . I'm his secretary."
He said, "Aw c'mon. Just reach across your desk, turn your
nameplate around and tell me it says, 'I'm his secretary.' " After
she stopped laughing, she volunteered, "My name is Barbara."
Wayne got through.

A little creative humor can take the big chill out of cold
calls. Once you get people laughing, you overcome their natural
inclination to hang up or say no. Like the time Wayne said he
was calling from an insurance agency. The prospect shot back,
"I don't need any insurance. And I don't like the fact that you're
calling me here. Please scratch me off your list." Wayne replied,
"Wow!" The prospect asked, "Wow, what?" Wayne said, "That
was 11 seconds. That must have been the fastest time you've
ever blown off a telemarketer."

The man started laughing and noted, "Yeah, I guess it is."
And Wayne said, "Too bad I kept you on the line, 'cause I just
ruined your record." Then the man really burst out laughing.
Wayne went in for the kill, "Hey, you've been on the phone for
over a minute, so now you've got to listen to my pitch." The
man listened and ended up buying insurance.

Do you need "insurance" when making cold calls? Then
make it a "policy" to get 'em laughing.

**"Creative salesmanship is finding a cure
for the common cold shoulder."**

—Anonymous

Son of Heating Up Cold Calls With Humor

To develop humor in cold calls, listen carefully to what the prospect says. That will give you an opportunity to be creative. Our sales humor hero, Wayne S., was selling insurance when he called the residence of George W. A woman answered the phone. Wayne asked, "Is George in?" Giggling, she said, "No, he's been dead for three years." Wayne quipped, "Well, I guess insurance for George is definitely out of the question!" She laughed heartily. When they finished talking, she purchased renter's insurance. Listening carefully gave him his opening.

Wayne was calling homes to sell construction tools. A little girl answered the phone. Wayne asked, "Is your dad there?" Wayne asked. She screamed, "Daddy!" When the father got on the line, Wayne said, "That's a pretty expensive intercom system you've got." Laughing, the father replied, "Yeah, she's quite an intercom." Wayne asked, "Are you paying her to be your secretary?" The father said, "No. Why?" Wayne shot back, "Because she's more efficient than a lot of forty-year-olds I know!" You guessed it—another sale rung up.

Not all humor has to be spontaneous. If you *expect* an objection, develop a funny line to defuse it. For example, many people tell telemarketers that they don't buy over the phone. Wayne surprises them by agreeing, "I don't either!" They usually laugh. Then he tells them why, "I sell over the phone all day," he explains. "I certainly don't want to talk to someone who's going to give me a pitch over the phone." By now he's begun to bond with the prospect, who becomes more willing to be friendly and listen. And that's no joke.

> **"Laughter is the shortest distance between two people."**
> **—Victor Borge**

Top Ten Reasons to Get 'Em Laughing

Charlie N., a commercial chemicals rep from Cleveland, is a big fellow with an equally girthed sense of humor. And he very successfully uses it to his sales advantage. Recently, he's been using the concept of late night television's David Letterman's *Top Ten List.* He creates his own series of them (called *"Pop Ten List"*) based around his company, products, and competitors. He uses them on sales calls, in presentations, in newsletters, and correspondence. Customers love it because he pokes clever, good-natured fun at himself, his company, and the other chemicals distributors in his territory. Here's one he did recently: *"Pop Ten Sales Lines Used by My Competitors:*

10. We promise—on our dead founder's grave—that we won't raise prices.
9. Is that a new pen in your pocket? Wanna try it out on our contract?
8. While you're reading our terms and conditions, mind if I chew on this burrito?
7. We'll throw in a free subscription to the *National Enquirer* if you order now!
6. Don't read the fine print—it's just a creative way to decorate the bottom of our contract.
5. If you don't sign now, we'll have the Islamic Jihad kidnap your cat.
4. And others. . . .

Charlie has created other amusing topics for his Pop Ten List, such as: "Brilliant Excuses We Give Our Customers," "Fascinating Things Overheard in Our Company's Restrooms," "Memorable Christmas Gifts We Give Our Customers," and "Playful Misprints on Our Contracts." Charlie's manager wrote one recently, "Ten Reasons Charlie Is the Best Salesperson in the Territory. " Can't top that!

"The most exciting phrase to hear in science, the one that heralds new discoveries, is not 'Eureka!' (I found it!) but "That's funny. . . . "

—Isaac Asimov

Defining the Situation

The way you define a problem or opportunity defines its solution.
Whether it's increasing sales, getting promoted, solving an account problem, changing employers, or finding a great place for lunch, you've got to focus on the clear and precise definition of what you'd like to accomplish.

When using creative thinking to solve a problem, first determine its *scope*. Do you want to fix a broad problem or focus on one of its narrower aspects? For example, "How can we reduce sales expenses?" gives you a wide latitude to develop answers. "What are some ideas to reduce administrative expenses?" narrows it down. Do you want to try to *mix* problems together or just concentrate on one? From what *perspective* will you consider the problem? Let's say you'd like to explore imaginative ways of increasing your sales. You can define your goal several different ways, each from a unique perspective. Here are some questions that will frame your solutions and ideas:

- What novel strategies can I use to fight our competitors?
- How can we get more new customers?
- How can we keep our customers from going to our competitors?
- How can we grab some of our competitor's customers away?
- How might we collaborate with other vendors to create more sales for everyone?

Notice how each question changes the slant on what you might want to accomplish.

"Success in solving a problem depends on choosing the right aspect, on attacking the fortress from its accessible side."
—George Polya

Some Thought Starters

CATEGORIES						
1	*2*	*3*	*4*	*5*	*6*	*7*
LET'S CONSIDER	WOULDN'T IT BE GREAT IF	HOW CAN WE	IN WHAT WAYS MIGHT WE	WHAT I'D LIKE TO SEE HAPPEN IS	I WONDER HOW WE COULD	HOW TO

Thought Starters!

T S!

You're psyched up and raring to maximize your creativity. There's just one little item—how do you start? With so many possibilities and opportunities, it's easy to become overwhelmed. You may feel like a mosquito in a nudist camp—you know what to do, but you don't know where to begin. Don't worry. It's easy.

Start by thinking about areas in your company's operations or customer environment that could benefit from a dose of creative treatment. Brainstorm and come up with a list of things that need to be fixed or taken advantage of. Want an effective technique to identify those possibilities? You can prime your creative pump by using thought-starter statements with "completer" words. Example: *"How can we* (thought-starter) *speed up* ("completer") responses to customer inquiries?" (desired goal or problem to solve)

Here are some *thought starters* to use:

"Let's consider . . ." or "Wouldn't it be great if . . .?"

"How can we . . .?" "In what ways might we . . .?" or "What I'd like to see happen is. . . . "

"I wonder how we could . . .? or How to . . .?"

Fill in those starters with *"completer"* words such as the following (then add on the problem or situation description you are working on):

correct	improve	change
resolve	fix	reduce
tap into	overcome	maximize
minimize	adopt	grab
optimize	speed up	exceed
accomplish	create	outsmart
eliminate	impress	win

Getting started properly will make your job a lot easier.

"Problems are only opportunities with thorns on them."

—Hugh Miller

Thinking About Thinking

What specific sales and service situations will benefit from your extra creative touches? What should you be thinking about to generate ideas to boost sales and customer satisfaction? Here are some *general* problem-solving or improvement-seeking questions:

- ❀ What (sales and service) activities or tasks do I perform that I want to improve upon?
- ❀ How can I make my selling easier and better?
- ❀ What are some ideal objectives to reach for?
- ❀ What would "delight" my customers?
- ❀ What new opportunities should I consider focusing on?

For example, if you're a salesperson in an auto/truck dealership, here are some *specific* questions based upon those five categories:

- ❀ How can we get people to trust us much more?
- ❀ How might I close more sales easier and faster?
- ❀ How can we get prospects outside of those who walk into our dealership?
- ❀ In what ways can we minimize complaints?
- ❀ How can we make potential buyers feel immediately welcome?
- ❀ How can we "earn" more referrals?
- ❀ In what ways can we outsmart and outsell our competitors beyond the "price thing"?
- ❀ What can we do that would dramatically set us apart from other auto/truck dealerships?
- ❀ How can we "entice" more people to visit our store?
- ❀ How can we practically guarantee keeping "customers for life"?
- ❀ What would impress our customers while depressing our competitors?
- ❀ What are we doing that we shouldn't be doing (at least in public anyway)?

"As is your sort of mind, so is your sort of search; you'll find what you desire."
—Robert Browning

Brainstorming...
Idea Forming

The goal of brainstorming is to produce *lots* of ideas *quickly*. You create ideas in phase one; you evaluate them in phase two. Assemble a group of five to ten people from diverse backgrounds who are interested in the situation for which you're developing ideas. Have them shout out ideas. A neutral "facilitator" (who does *not* submit ideas) writes their suggestions on a flipchart. Pages can be removed and taped to a wall for later reference.

Encourage participants to come up with original ideas. They can also "piggyback" on the ideas of others by creating variations of someone else's idea. Keep the atmosphere fun, energetic, supportive, and nonjudgmental. Make the first five minutes a "silly session" where nothing but crazy, funny, and outlandish ideas are tossed around. This helps rid people of their inhibitions.

The *rules of brainstorming* are:

* Call out ideas in a rapid-fire, free-flowing fashion; don't think about or censor your ideas. Just shout out what immediately comes to mind.
* Don't squelch, discuss, evaluate, or judge ideas during phase one of idea generation.
* Welcome all ideas—even those that are far out. Don't try to be "practical" since even wild and wacky ideas can get others to think of more down-to-earth ones.
* Set a number goal of ideas to be reached (30–40 ideas) or a specific time period (30–45 minutes) for the idea-generating phase.
* In phase two, evaluate the ideas based upon chosen criteria (time, money, technical considerations, etc.). Then rank ideas in priority based on criteria of judgment.

"Analysis kills spontaneity. The grain once ground into flour springs and germinates no more."

—Henri Frederic Amiel

Great Grazing
and Gazing

When stimulated with rich visual material—pictures, symbols, illustrations, or objects, our brain can suddenly ignite a idea for a problem or opportunity we're working on. *Grazing* gives your brain visual raw material to stimulate ideas. The technique is to let your eyes roam in a passing manner at various things without looking for anything specific. Keep your mind open and don't try mentally to force connections. Just look without expecting or "searching" for anything. Be open. Here are some great (image-rich) idea pastures to graze in:

Library or Bookstore. Browse magazines and books with lots of pictures and images. For example, books on architecture, graphic or product design, and photography provide a fertile feeding ground for the eyes and mind. What idea connections can you make from these?

Museums and art galleries. Study paintings, sculptures, and other art works and nature exhibits. Read the accompanying descriptions about them. What do they remind you of? What is unique and clever about them?

Supermarkets and department stores. Walk around curiously scanning the diverse products on shelves and in departments. Look at the advertising, decoration, the products themselves, and the way they are displayed. What suddenly sparks your curiosity or interest?

If you find something that grabs your attention, then *gaze* at it. Intently study it with interest and wonder. Look at its shapes, colors, textures, and overall design and function. What does it make you think of or feel? What offshoot ideas can you get from it? Simple as it sounds, grazing and gazing can be amazing!

"The soul never thinks without a picture."
—Aristotle

"Driven" by Ideas to Excel

Bud V. decided to go on a grazing and gazing trip to a new shopping mall north of Houston. Browsing from store to store, he looked with curious interest in the hope of having some unexpected sales ideas sprout up. Bud had recently started his own investment consulting firm and was an avid hobbyist and "tinkerer." His grazing took him through toy, hobby, confectionery, and electronics/gadget stores, among others.

Zap! A clever synthesis of several things pieced itself together in an instant the following day while he was running. For three months he'd been unsuccessful in all his conventional attempts to see Tyler C., a wealthy and influential business leader. One reason was Tyler's staunchly protective long-time "gatekeeper," Rita J. She deftly and swiftly parried the persuasive thrusts of eager salespeople requesting an audience with Mr. C. Bud, who's seldom hesitated going "outside the box," decided to try a bold "theatrical" approach.

At the mall, he bought a radio-controlled model truck, a walkie-talkie, some Godiva chocolates, and parts from the hobby store. He built a tiny trailer to be pulled by the truck and hid the miniature walkie-talkie inside. On the trailer, he placed the chocolates next to a folded card that had typing on it and Rita's name on the front. Out of view, he directed his remote control truck/trailer to Rita. Over his walkie-talkie, he announced, "Ms. J., a delivery for you. Will you accept? Please reply." Since the trailer's walkie-talkie was in an open position to send *and* receive, Bud had a brief conversation with the startled Rita. Bud jokingly announced the candy as a "sweet bribe." She read the card, which said, "If you feel I've been this creative to reach Mr. C, I'll be even more resourceful in helping him in six specific financial areas." Bud took a risk. The gate was thrown open!

"Anybody who is any good is different from anybody else."

—Felix Frankfurter

Do You "Prop Up" Your Sales?

Props can be powerful creative tools to make your sales points l-e-a-p o-u-t at your customers. Numerous studies have shown that using the proper visual aids and props will make sales messages more persuasive and memorable. Harold L. used props for persuasive effect. He was a sales engineer for a lubricants company that had a major breakthrough—an expensive, but incredibly "slippery" lubricant that reduced friction more than 90% over other advanced products.

During presentations to groups of customers, Harold would show highly magnified slides of steel surfaces that looked jagged. "Picture raw surfaces rubbing against each other," he would say as he asked them to take two pieces of very coarse grit sandpaper and rub together. The scratchy, noisy friction was dramatically felt by customers. "Now spread product 'X' (his competitor's lubricant) on the coarse sandpaper," he requested. They did and felt much less resistance when rubbing the sheets together. Harold then gave them new pieces of extremely fine grit sandpaper. He asked them to spread his company's radically new lubricant on the sheets and rub them together.

The difference was amazing! There was almost no sensation of friction. "It's like rubbing air against air," he metaphorically quipped. His impressed customers thought it was pretty "slick." Think about what *meaningful* props (even everyday ones) you can use to add some reality, curiosity, dramatics, and persuasive muscle to your presentations/demonstrations. Then, watch how your sales will be substantially "propped up."

> **"Lots of people know a good thing the minute the other fellow sees it first."**
> **—Joe E. Hedges**

Is Your Creative Selling an Illusion?

Imagine being a "sales prestidigitator" who could make competitors dissolve right before your customer's eyes or who could levitate sales contracts in midair. You can fantasize, can't you? Actually, you can use one of the most creative forms of grabbing someone's attention—magic! That's exactly what Bill Schmeelk, founder of Wellington Enterprises, an illusion company, does. Besides creating mega-tricks for superstars such as David Copperfield and Harry Blackstone, he's created mechanisms and ingenious precision-made props for companies such as IBM, Chrysler, General Motors, and also for many small (budget-minded) firms. He's designed selling-point illusions to use at sales meetings, trade shows, and other sales events. He's made executives disappear on stage and suspended women on vinyl siding for an industry show. Schmeelk created a scenario where a (preselected and briefed) audience member of a sales convention, for example, is "randomly picked" to come up on stage. Suddenly his tie gets caught in the wringer of a machine he's supposed to demonstrate and he's then pulled in and spit out flat as a pancake!

For one liquor beverage company, Bill created a card trick for all salespeople to use when they visited a new store. The goal was to get buyers involved in a presentation and to have them remember the new product. A buyer was handed three cards—two jacks and an ace. The salesperson turned them upside down and had the buyer take out the ace. The two jacks were then shown. When the buyer looked at what he thought would naturally be the ace, he saw a picture of the new product! You don't have to be a "Sales Houdini" to begin learning small magic tricks that might be used professionally to reinforce your sales points. Perhaps "abracadabra" or "hocus-pocus" might become a new sales close!

> **"Within you right now is the power to do things you never dreamed possible. This power becomes available to you just as soon as you change your beliefs."**
> **—Maxwell Maltz**

A Magically Marvelous Sales Presentation

"Idea Wizard" is Walter N.'s new nickname. Here's why. Walter sells factory automation equipment to manufacturers. He was assigned a new account with great potential, but a competitor was favored in a large upcoming deal. Walter felt he had to brew up a high risk/high gain strategy using an unorthodox approach to make a calculated "dramatic impact" on his customers.

Walter gave a one-hour sales presentation (highlighting his solution) to fourteen decision makers. The presentation included dazzling visuals designed by a computer multimedia expert. Three-dimensional animation impressively showed how Walter's equipment would innovate his customer's operation. Video shots of the present operation were mixed with segments from 1940s comedy movies to highlight critical points needed to clinch the sale. Operated from a laptop computer and LCD projector, this action-oriented presentation made his major competitor's 35mm slide presentation appear lifeless. But Walter had one more "trick up his sleeve"—a professional magician!

Hired to play the role of Walter's "partner," the magician knew just what to do. Asking the chief financial officer of the company to step forward during the presentation, the magician started pulling "real" $1,000 bills from the man's clothing. After he gathered fourteen bills, they caught fire in his hand. "That's how much money you'll burn every quarter if you choose any other equipment!" he bellowed. The magician used other tricks to make Walter's remaining key points highly memorable. It worked beautifully. Favoritism for his competitor suddenly "disappeared."

"People will pay more to be entertained than educated."
                                          —Johnny Carson

Navigate Ideas
With Mind
Mapping

Casey Stengel said, "If you don't know where you're going, you might end up somewhere else." He would have loved *mind mapping*.* Creativity expert Tony Buzan developed this powerful way to capture ideas, to plan, or solve problems. It ensures you'll know where you're going creatively. Mind mapping generates more and better ideas faster than traditional outlining techniques because you diagram ideas, the relationships between them, and all their details on a single sheet of paper. Because it involves visually enticing elements of color, images/symbols, and key words, it speeds understanding and helps memorization.

Michael J. Gelb, an expert mind mapper and President of High Performance Learning®, a creativity training company in Great Falls, Virginia, gives these tips on how to mind map:

1. Draw a representative image/picture of your topic in the middle of a large sheet of paper positioned horizontally. Use two to three colored pens to highlight it.

2. *Print* key words over lines that radiate outward from your central image. Connect lines to reflect your free-flowing, spontaneous outpouring of ideas. Use symbols, graphics/illustrations, pictures, and colors to have critical concepts vividly appear whenever possible. For example, ideas might be colored, based on topic or importance. Numbers, exclamation points, or other symbols (such as dingbats) can focus on or clarify relationships and meanings.

3. Review your drawing after you've finished your thoughts. Consider adding or realigning arrows/lines to modify idea connections, using new pictures, symbols, and colors to finish your map, and eliminating extraneous items. Map it, baby; turn yourself into an "idea cartographer."

> **"The idea is there, locked inside. All you have to do is remove the excess stone."**
> **—Michelangelo**

---

* Mind mapping and HPL are registered trademarks of the Buzan and Gelb Organizations, respectively.

Develop a Head for a Metaphor

Metaphors are words or phrases in which a concept or object, for example, is likened to another *as if it were* the other. The right metaphor can take a complex idea and elegantly simplify it. Descriptive metaphors can visually paint an idea in a vivid and memorable way. They can get people to look at themselves and situations they're facing in new and insightful ways and set the stage for dramatic change.

"Computer virus," for example, is a metaphor that enables people nontechnically to visualize how computers get *infected* by *bugs* and how it can *spread*. "Thinking aerobics" is a metaphor we use to describe exercising your mind by doing creative problem-solving puzzles. "Intellectual assets" is a popular metaphor for symbolizing the value of people's brainpower.

Creative salesperson Sandra E. worked for a Minneapolis firm providing temporary employees. One of her customers was experiencing a painful and oppressive increase in administrative work due to rapid growth. Sandra poignantly summarized how her firm could help: "With our trained team, we'll provide a *Heimlich maneuver* for all the choking paperwork that's threatening to kill your success." That compelling visual and psychological metaphor she used "coughed up" a sale for her. The best metaphors are short, simple, and stimulate a person's feelings, thoughts, and actions. Use metaphors to think of new sales strategies, marketing messages, problem definitions, and other applications that require a new and exciting perspective.

"Metaphors are word pictures that give language power and richness by involving our senses in the experience."
—Gabriele Lusser Rico

A Metaphor
That's Better
For . . .

Sales prodigy Rhonda D. helped her small software company skyrocket its customer service image by developing a clever metaphor—*U.S.A. (United States of Action)*. Her goal was to communicate a new customer service concept that played off the best elements of our country's beliefs, values, and philosophies. Each word in the metaphor had a distinct meaning: "United" meant teamwork. Company employees worked closely with each other and their customers. They were united for one overriding purpose—to provide unmatched customer service. A map of the United States was created and divided into six *"States"* of conscious customer service: (1) readiness, (2) willingness, (3) competence, (4) cooperation, (5) dedication, and (6) innovation.

On this colorful map (which is given to customers), descriptive information told how these six states operated for the benefit of the customer. Finally, the word *"Action"* symbolized the dynamic focus of their customer operations. Extending the metaphor, a *Constitution* was framed that listed the inspired principles under which the company would strive for customer service excellence. A *Declaration of Independence* was also written. In it, the company declared that it would forever free itself from the commonplace business "tyranny" of mediocrity, complacency, inefficiency, and errors. This multipart metaphor helped the company's employees to focus upon key concepts. And the patriotic undertones reassured customers that they were in good hands.

"How sweet it is to stand on the edge of tomorrow."

—Robert Schuller

Attribute Listing

Attribute listing is a creativity tool that is especially useful for designing/redesigning something (products, services, proposals, etc.). It can also help solve sales problems, modify plans and strategies, and give lots of variations to ideas. Attribute listing "reinvents" or enhances something by adding and combining bits and pieces from numerous sources.

First, list all the *current* features or characteristics of the product, situation, or idea you are working on. Second, below each attribute, list as many *alternatives* as you can think of. Third, look at the *possibilities* you have for picking and choosing one from each column (as the circles show in the example). Fourth, *assemble* these combinations into a new form. Suppose you were trying to design a new type of a ballpoint pen. The following chart shows how to lay out attribute listing.

Present Attributes of Model #5AZ Ballpoint Pen

Shape	Construction	Cartridge	Mechanism	Size
round	plastic body	steel ink	push button	6" long

Alternate Attributes

Shape	Construction	Cartridge	Mechanism	Size
hex	metal	plastic	twisting	3"–12" (extendible)
square	wood	no cartridge	gravity fed	
beaded	glass	paper	shaken	
twisted	paper	refillable	flip	Various fixed lengths
sculptured	rubber	multiple inks	auto feed	
custom	ceramic	solid ink	pull	

The new pen design has a beaded shape made out of a ceramic material. It has a paper ink cartridge, is pulled to get the tip out, and is extendible. Use the same technique for changing sales letters, proposals, presentations, account plans, marketing strategies, and numerous other activities, as some of the following pages illustrate.

"An idea is a feat of association."
—Robert Frost

Happy "C.A.M.P.E.R.S."

Creativity involves doing something differently. *Changing* or *manipulating* a product, service, process, operation, or design is at the very heart of creativity and innovation. C.A.M.P.E.R.S. is an acronym representing the primary ways to change something. Advertising great Alex Osborn made this type of technique well known. Here's what it stands for:

Combine? What different (perhaps seemingly unrelated) ideas, concepts, designs, parts, elements, strategies, or other things can you combine to create something new?

Adapt? What parts can you adapt—"borrow"—from places, people, things, or other fields to enhance your selling and service? What ideas can you use from sports, philosophy, military, religion, architecture, entertainment, advertising, or engineering to fit your sales situations?

Modify? How can you change something (a proposal, strategy, etc.) by making it bigger/smaller, faster/slower, giving it a new twist, altering its shape, packaging, message, style?

Put to other uses? What novel, new, and clever uses or applications might you find for your products and services? Besides your traditional customers, who else might find creative uses for your product or service?

Eliminate? What can you reduce, simplify, delete, or streamline from the way you sell that would improve sales efficiency and service?

Rearrange? How can you reschedule, change the order, interchange parts, or transpose things to create new alternatives?

Substitute? What materials, methods, people, concepts, techniques, or places can you replace with the ones you're now using?

"Fundamental progress has to do with the reinterpretation of basic ideas."
—Alfred North Whitehead

Far-Out
Sales Proposal

Most sales proposals are fairly "traditional." They're written in a no-nonsense, dry, fact-filled way. Not too imaginative. Michael D., an account manager for a personal computer manufacturer, decided it was time for him to cross over to the "far side" and be creative with his proposal.

His proposals, heavily text-laden and about eighty pages long, were ponderous and not very interesting to read or view. His goal was to make them more inviting—to transform them from dull business documents into creative sales communication tools that would stand out from those of his competitors. Using attribute listing and C.A.M.P.E.R.S., he:

- ✸ Reduced eighty pages to forty (a lot of the content was found to be extraneous boilerplate).
- ✸ Added more illustrations to break up the text and help understanding.
- ✸ Reversed the format from 8½ × 11" vertical to horizontal with two columns and had it plastic spiral-bound.
- ✸ Modified the design by providing more white space between text to make it more uncluttered and less intimidating to read.
- ✸ Added clip art cartoons with custom captions to make major points stick out.
- ✸ Replaced the white cover with a classy-looking blue one.
- ✸ Cleverly titled it: "A Marriage Proposal" with sections on "Prenuptial Agreement," "The Ceremony," "Living Happily Ever After," and "Housekeeping Rules" that replaced traditional sections such as "Terms and Conditions." The marriage metaphor showed that his company viewed the customer relationship as a long-term commitment to be respected and nurtured. Last we heard, the honeymoon was still on!

"The thing that makes a creative person is to be creative and that is all there is to it."
—Edward Albee

Is This a
Sales Letter or
What?

A weak sales letter is defined by the three m's: a *mess* that *misses* the *masses*. LaTisha W., a sales manager for a photocopier manufacturer, wanted to avoid this pitfall. She wanted a new introductory sales letter that would immediately grab the readers' interest and make it easier for sales reps to get appointments. Her design goal was a brief, attractive, personalized, meaningful, and persuasive letter. And it had to be creative and tasteful—unlike any mediocre sales letter.

Here's what the new letter was like:

❀ It was a standard $8\frac{1}{2} \times 11$-inch size but folded in half. The heavy card stock paper, which could be output to a desktop *color* printer, was richly designed to look like an invitation on the outside. The prospect's name was printed in front using a classy script font in gold color. Other text was printed in blue.

❀ When the one-page letter was opened, a pop-up color cartoon unfolded (a special perforated paper was used). The cartoon related to a photocopy operation. Via word processing, the customer's name and a personalized comment with the key sales point directly below it were included.

❀ Humor and fascinating statistics were used in each of the three key selling benefits that were designed to motivate the reader to agree to a meeting.

❀ Special stick-it notes were printed with a picture of their latest copier and stuck to the letter with the salesperson's name on it.

❀ As an incentive to meet, the letter promised to give the prospect a booklet titled, *150 Ways Your Copier Can Add Creativity to Your Business*. LaTisha is now jokingly called "CreativeWoman." She loves it!

"We make way for the man who boldly pushes past us."

—Christian Nestell Bovee

Hey, What's the Big Idea?

Aleta S., a sales engineer for an electronics automation company, spotted an impressive-looking large drawing coming out of a new printer as she walked through her marketing department. Always on the lookout for ideas, she was intrigued with the new device. It could scan an $8\frac{1}{2} \times 11$-inch original and create an enlargement size from 23×31 inches up to 45×59 inches. Or it could output from a personal computer. "Hmmm . . . how could I use that?" she wondered.

"Blueprint" suddenly popped into her mind. "That's it," she thought, "I'll create a *big idea blueprint* for Glenda J." Glenda J. was a prospect whose company was engineering a breakthrough technology mag-lev train. Glenda had asked vendors how they might conceptually implement an innovative quick-pay-and-enter system for their train. And Aleta wanted her solution to stand out.

Using a takeoff on the "Yellow Brick Road," Aleta had a graphic artist create a large spectacular visual from the new printer called "The Yellow Brick Track." It was a creative map plan with a stylized picture of the ultramodern mag-lev train. It showed the path of the train reaching each station as a sequential event that would occur during the implementation of her company's electronic entry systems.

With her large "blueprint" in hand, Aleta had one more task. She wanted to involve Glenda in the ceremonial unfurling of the "blueprint" on the meeting room table. "Can you give me a hand uncurling this plan I've put together for you?" Aleta asked. As Glenda unrolled the plan, she saw the engineer on top of the train was a caricature of *her* and laughed uproariously. The sale was now definitely on track!

"I had a monumental idea this morning, but I didn't like it."

—Samuel Goldwyn

Your Code of Creativity

Want to maximize your use of creativity in work and life? Then develop your own special *code of creativity*. Within it, include your feelings, values, philosophy, and objectives, as well as anything else that will motivate you to become more imaginative. Here's an example of a code Marcia W. (insurance saleswoman) wrote and signed. She posted it in both her office and home:

Marcia's Code of Creativity

I, the Undersigned Will . . .

1. Use my imagination as often as possible, not just for special or demanding situations.
2. Have more fun toying with new and radical ideas.
3. Not judge my creativity against that of others, but upon how creative I can be.
4. Go outside my comfort zone to grow more.
5. Laugh more and not take myself as seriously as before.
6. Encourage creativity from my co-workers.
7. Not belittle myself for making mistakes and having setbacks; I'll learn from them.
8. Celebrate my creative accomplishments (especially with chocolate!).
9. Value even small ideas that I come up with.
10. Become an optimistic "possibility, no-limits thinker."
11. Use my creativity to help my family, my community, and society.
12. Always try to be open-minded and listen to the ideas and suggestions of others.
13. Not become defensive when my ideas are not accepted.
14. Break boring and useless old habits and be more adventurous.
15. Take greater risks and not regret doing it.

Hint: Post the code where you see it often—refrigerator, bathroom, sock drawer.

"No man can produce great things who is not thoroughly sincere in dealing with himself."

—James Russell Lowell

Last-Minute
Fueling Tips

Before you head off to the "service station" that follows, here are some key reminders to help fill your creative tank to the top:

- ✸ Realize that you have lots of creative potential that you can tap into and use for great results.
- ✸ Develop a passion for unusual ideas and new experiences.
- ✸ Be creative every day, even in small ways. Make imaginative thinking a successful strong habit.
- ✸ Take more calculated risks. Your life will positively change!
- ✸ Don't let success make you complacent. Always seek better ways to do your job.
- ✸ Brush off the criticism others may have of your ideas. They may be ignorant of their value, jealous, or threatened. Surge ahead anyway!
- ✸ Keep laughing, keep smiling, keep joking.
- ✸ Through your creativity, turn stumbling blocks into building blocks.
- ✸ Never give in, never give up.
- ✸ Hang around positive, optimistic, can-do, action-oriented people; avoid nay-sayers and doom-and-gloomers whose negativity easily rubs off.
- ✸ Develop a clear vision, dream, and plan for your attractive future. Use creativity to guide and help control your exciting destiny.
- ✸ Develop a thick skin with mistakes. Don't beat yourself up, lose confidence, or dwell in regret. Creativity, failing, and making mistakes are inextricably linked.
- ✸ Use creativity and humor to have fun with your customers. Both of you will love it!
- ✸ Countless ideas are waiting to be implemented. Don't discount your idea by believing, "If it *could* have been done and *should* have been done, it *would* have been done." Do it now!
- ✸ Wake up that "sleeping giant thinking organ" between your ears!

"Before everything else, getting ready is the secret of success."
—Henry Ford

Service Station

PREMIUM

FILL-ER-UP?

"Fill'er up" with ideas, information, and tools:

Pump 1: Self-Assessment and Plan—Getting Your Creativity Fired Up

Pump 2: Applying Creativity—Questions, Ideas, and Resources

Pump 3: Word-to-Idea Trigger List—A Useful Tool to Spark Your Imagination

Pump 4: Fun and Play at Work—Checklist of 100 Ideas to Amuse and Use

Pump 5: Book List—Suggested Reading

Pump 1:
Self-Assessment and Plan—Getting
Your Creativity Fired Up

By writing in your answers after each question in this section, you can help to assess and analyze your creativity status and potential for application. This will get you thinking and acting upon factors affecting your imagination power. This section also has a planning component to enable you to focus your creative efforts for maximum results.

Consider using this section for discussion of sales creativity during sales meetings, training workshops, or other events.

1. How would you define "SALES CREATIVITY"?

   _____

   _____

   _____

2. When was the *last time* you came up with any kind of "creative" sales or service idea? (check box)
   ☐ today
   ☐ last week
   ☐ last year
   ☐ yesterday
   ☐ last month
   ☐ can't remember

3. Describe the idea and explain what you felt was creative about it.

   _____

   _____

   _____

4. Why is creativity important (or *not* important) to you in your job or life, in general?

_____

_____

_____

5. Describe the traits and behaviors of several creative people you *personally* know.

_____

_____

_____

6. List several reasons why *you* consider yourself creative (if not, explain why).

_____

_____

_____

7. Describe the specific conditions (times, locations, activities, feelings, social situations, surrounding atmosphere, people you're with, etc.) when you are usually your *most* creative.

_____

_____

_____

8. How can you be *even more* creative in the future?

_____

_____

_____

9. What's preventing you from using all your creative potential on the job *right now?*

_____

_____

_____

10. I consider myself to be (check the appropriate box):
    ☐ *high* risk-taker
    ☐ *minimal* risk-taker
    ☐ *moderate* risk-taker
    ☐ *non*risk-taker
    Explain why you see yourself as *that type* of risk-taker.

    _____

    _____

    _____

11. In what areas of work or life would you like to change by taking more risks and why?

    _____

    _____

    _____

12. What are some reasons that are *preventing you* from taking more "calculated" risks (e.g., what do you fear would be the drawbacks or consequences of your risk-taking)?

    _____

    _____

    _____

13. Describe some strategies to prompt you to take *more risks* now and in the future.

    _____

    _____

    _____

14. What customer or internal problems would best lend themselves to a creative problem-solving approach? List them in priority order.

    _____

    _____

    _____

15. What three to five sales activities (e.g., prospecting, giving presentations, developing competitive strategies, etc.) will you begin applying more creativity to? List them in the order that you will start focusing on.

   _____

   _____

   _____

16. In what ways can your manager permit (or motivate) you to use more of your creative abilities?

   _____

   _____

   _____

17. What are some ideas you have on making your sales organization and its culture and climate more creative and fun overall?

   _____

   _____

   _____

Pump 2:
Applying Creativity—Questions, Ideas, and Resources

This *very important section* contains items to help you further develop your creativity and apply it in selling. The following questions (with some examples) will help you or a sales and service team to select problems or opportunities to work on. Look through this list and decide which are priority ones to

which you might apply creative thinking tools. Most importantly, use this question checklist as an idea-jogger for yourself to
create your own list of problem-solving or opportunity-seeking
topics to work on. We've also included ideas and information
about sources to spark your thinking and products and resources
to use throughout your selling activities.

Use the following questions to work on ways to enhance
each aspect of your sales activities. Your sales manager might
select one or more of these questions to brainstorm ideas at each
scheduled sales meeting. In this way, your sales organization
can regularly come up with ideas that can benefit everyone and
make for an interesting meeting as well.

1. What metaphors can you create to describe your competitive situation in a new light and from a fresh new perspective?
What metaphors might compare you and your competitor in
terms of size, operation, philosophy, strengths/weaknesses, customer service policies, employees, etc.? *Example:* your competitor
is a large, slow moving elephant; your company is a fast, nimble,
hungry tiger.

2. How can you more creatively get energized and motivated each day to face new prospects and new challenges?

3. In what ways might you better use desktop publishing
to improve your sales and service materials? How can you make
better visual aids, brochures, sales letters, training materials, proposals, etc.? How might you make more imaginative use of the
following:

- Clip art (including cartoons).
- Computer scanners. What pictures, images, or illustrations from magazines (especially old-time ones), books,
  newspapers, or flyers can you scan into your computer
  (check copyrights)?
- Design layout templates to make materials more attractive and easier to read.
- Color printers and copiers in your office.
- Stock images from CD-ROMs, including people and personalities, lifestyles, backgrounds/textures, places, para-
  phernalia, or "weird" scenes.

Image Club Graphics is a good source for clip art/stock images to make your sales materials (e.g., presentation visual aids) more creative. Order their catalog from Image Club Graphics, Inc., c/o Publisher's Mail Service, 10545 West Donges Court, Milwaukee, WI 53224-9967 (1-800-661-9410).

4. How can you cleverly recruit, entice, or "invite" customers away from your competitors?

5. What can you do to take more prudent risks (that might bring high gains) without feeling the self-guilt of failing or the possibility of being "punished"? What types of risks would give the best return on your "investment of guts"?

6. How can you get people favorably—even enthusiastically—to respond to you in cold call situations?

7. Where and how else can you get more qualified sales leads faster?

8. In what ways can you better use "good" humor in selling and servicing your customers? For example, how might humor help you to get appointments, handle upset customers, demonstrate your product, address concerns, and describe your competitors in an amusing, less-than-attractive way that is nonoffensive to your customer?

One great software program to get you started is Quotes on Line, which is DOS-based and contains more than 12,000 quotes—many from off-beat sources and extremely funny. It is available from askSam Systems at 800–800–1997.

9. In what ways can you take care of your administrative paperwork faster, better, and less expensively? What can be eliminated, streamlined, or improved?

10. What are some ideas on getting more positive and *free* public relations and advertising for your company and its products and services?

11. How might you team up with other individuals, companies, associations, or other organizations to work together in mutually beneficial ways? What types of strategic alliances might work best?

12. How can your office's customer database design and operation be more up-to-date, accurate, and otherwise helpful to sales and service people?

13. What ideas can you come up with to make your direct mail marketing more efficient, attractive, convincing, and inexpensive? What might improve the response ratio?

14. Does your sales group have vision and mission statements? If so, how can you creatively use them in sales situations?

15. How might you transform your relationship with your customers from buyer/seller to strong "partners"? How else might you improve the personal and professional bond between you and your customer? How can you "lock up" your customer's business?

16. How might your sales group collaborate with some companies whose products or services might complement yours (e.g., joint advertising, trade shows, seminars)?

17. What are some imaginative ways to deal more effectively with the frequent rejection experienced in selling and motivate yourself to make more sales calls?

18. What interesting ways can you thank your customer for doing business with you and your company—ways that are remembered and appreciated by the customer?

19. How can a sales account team be more *effective and efficient* in working the account? How might everyone work in a more synchronized way, for example?

20. What new sources and channels of networking might produce surprising numbers of new leads and qualified prospects?

21. How can you make it easier and more conducive/attractive/beneficial for your present customers to introduce you to others who might be buyers?

22. How might you ingeniously use a facsimile machine to help out in selling and customer service (e.g., fax on demand)?

23. Where and how in your selling cycle can you *entertain or amuse* your prospects? What planned activities might you hold in your office, off-site, or at the customer's office, for example? What funny (off-the-shelf or customized) cards might you send with an amusing message? What else can you do to get them laughing and signing?

24. What can you do to dress and groom yourself in very distinctive, but always tasteful and appropriate ways such that you "stand out without sticking out"? For example, what high-quality accessories can you use to enhance your individual image? What special phrases or motto would make you remembered? What notable things like a special signature, calling card, or other behaviors might be appropriate professional "trademarks" that set you apart from the usual crowd of competitors?

25. What novel ways can you more effectively motivate prospects on the telephone to give you an appointment to first meet with them?

26. Besides brochures and other product literature, how else can your sales group communicate (in an exciting way) the features and benefits of your products and services? For example, audiocassettes, videotapes, computer diskettes, CD-ROMs, faxes, messengers, Internet, etc.?

27. In what ways can your sales meetings be made more fun, interesting, learning-oriented, interactive, and (overall) productive?

28. How can you get more prospects to come to *your* sales office instead of you calling on them?

29. How can you make your store or office more conducive to buying or otherwise doing business there?

30. How can you develop a super-effective sixty-second sales presentation that covers critical points persuasively enough to get the prospect's interest to proceed further?

31. How can salespeople and sales managers better work *together* to:

⊛ Provide career growth opportunities?
⊛ Do forecasting/planning?
⊛ Improve internal operations?
⊛ Make joint sales calls more effective?
⊛ Solve problems faster?
⊛ Improve customer service?
⊛ Develop new competitive sales strategies?

32. What are some ways to make your trial closes and closes more entertaining, interesting, and effective? For example, one

jovial salesperson who sells advertising for a local magazine had a picture taken with fifteen neighborhood children (who were told to "look sad") and printed it on the back of his business card, which he jokingly handed to the prospect when he wanted to close the sale. Looking at all the exaggeratedly grim faces, and reading the caption, "Help . . . I've got to feed them!" made buyers laughingly more receptive to buy.

33. How can you creatively strengthen the image of your company especially compared to your competitors? How can your company be portrayed as being more of an innovator, problem solver, industry leader, technology giant, or whatever other traits/images are desired?

34. In what resourceful (but ethical) ways might you get past the "gatekeeper" to speak with a potential buyer?

35. How can you make your live product demonstrations more realistic, interesting, impacting, persuasive, and entertaining? How can you get your customers more involved in the demonstrations? How can you creatively give a dynamic team demonstration with other sales or support professionals? How might another customer (from a different company) help you out and give persuasive support? How can you add relevant "showmanship" to it?

36. How can you get other people (friends, family, neighbors, business acquaintances, even strangers) to somehow "sell" for you? What types of physical or psychological rewards would encourage people to give you leads, set up meetings with prospects, or otherwise assist you in identifying opportunities and closing the sale?

37. What ideas, concepts, techniques, or clever phrases can you borrow from television sitcoms, movies, commercials, game shows, or documentaries that you might use in your sales and service activities?

38. In what ways might you use professional entertainers to help your sales organization's efforts? For example, how might comedians, magicians, singers, actors, impersonators, newscasters/reporters, or other personalities/celebrities give your group ideas to beat competitors, entertain customers, endorse your products, "schmooze" with customers at trade shows, help

design punchy sales messages and materials, or participate at large group sales presentations?

39. Where can you get ideas in a large public or university library? For example:

- ✸ What popular magazines should you scan for topics or interesting titles?
- ✸ What business or technical periodicals/reports should you look at?
- ✸ What book topics should you consider?
- ✸ What references (i.e., *Business Periodicals Index*) should you browse through looking for trigger words?
- ✸ What types and sources of statistical information might prove interesting?
- ✸ What databases should you check out?

40. What are some creative ways to use the *Internet* to locate leads, qualify prospects, spread your sales messages, and open up new channels of marketing? How might you elicit more creative ideas on selling your products or services from other users on the *Internet?*

41. What clever themes, perhaps in the form of acronyms, can you think of to tie into various parts of your sales activities?

42. How might you use "seminar selling" (pitching to groups of potential customers in a seminar environment) to improve sales productivity and efficiency? What ideas and techniques might you borrow from successful television *infomercials?*

43. What distinctive and creative phone answering messages might your sales organization consider using? What unusual music, humor, messages, etc., might your group consider for caller wait times?

44. How can creativity make your sales and service presentations more:

- ✸ Convincing, believable, and persuasive?
- ✸ Interesting, fascinating, eye-opening, entertaining, fun, and enjoyable?
- ✸ Attention-grabbing from the start?
- ✸ Motivating, positive, optimistic, or inspiring?

❋ Relevant—tightly focused on the customer's needs, wants, and priorities?

❋ Humorous and amusing?

❋ Benefit-focused (instead of feature-driven)?

❋ Interactive with the customer?

❋ Customized and personalized?

❋ Precise and accurate?

❋ Vividly memorable?

❋ Friendly, personable, sincere, and natural?

❋ Efficient in terms of time and energy?

❋ Appealing to the customer's beliefs, values, tastes, preferences, and attitudes?

❋ Solutions-focused and value-added?

❋ Competitive-busting?

❋ Persuasively climactic in its ending?

How can you break the dull, conventional mold of giving presentations? What novel formats might you use to communicate? What about using a clever (business) fairy tale or using nothing but customized cartoons for visual aids? Suppose you made part of a large group presentation into a play, skit, roast, or game show (perhaps with your audience participating)?

What poignant analogies or examples can you use to explain or describe complex, abstract, or otherwise difficult-to-understand things about your company's technology, products, services, contracts?

How might simple magic or bar tricks, puzzles, ice-breakers, optical illusions, or science project experiments help make a sales point *much* stronger? What ideas, humor, or messages can you get from the old (1930s–1950s) movies and radio broadcasts? How might you use clips from them in your presentations? From what magazines of that era (such as *Life, Look, Saturday Evening Post)* can you extract interesting pictures or other ideas (check copyrights).

What "props" might you use to add animation, drama, entertainment, or greatly strengthen and make more memorable your key sales points during a demonstration or presentation? What everyday objects might be cleverly employed to add theatrical persuasive power to your messages—to visually illustrate something? For example, how might you use such things as a fire extinguisher, food processor, flashlight, signs, sponges, bells, a battery operated toy, paint brushes, a portable vacuum cleaner, cookbooks, a rubber dart gun, a rope, a measuring stick, crutches, ball bearings, or any other of thousands of items?

45. What ideas can you think of to meet *higher level* decision makers compared to some of the prospects you are now meeting?

46. What are some inexpensive and useful "giveaways" to hand out/send to prospects that would help in the sales cycle?

47. If your sales organization has a "demo room" to showcase and demonstrate your products, how might it be imaginatively designed to create a stimulating climate, paint a realistic setting, or create a certain theme to support your product or service applications and benefits? *Examples:* Roman room, movie theater, war room, haunted house, museum, laboratory, repair shop, railroad station, or bridge of a starship? What sounds played in the background would give realism to your demo room? How can customers cleverly be greeted to set an expectant tone? What types of creative photos of "satisfied customers" might be displayed?

48. How can you act more like a true business consultant/advisor to your customers beyond your typical sales and service responsibilities? How can you creatively help solve the customer's problems, take advantage of opportunities, or help enhance his or her operations? How can you help him or her to be more innovative?

49. What types of stores or shops might you visit to buy things (e.g., props, supplies) to use or to graze and gaze in for ideas to use? (you never know from what everyday or unusual places great ideas may pop up). Here are some types of stores in which to look for creative ideas:

- ✪ Large supermarkets
- ✪ Department stores
- ✪ Consumer electronics/appliance stores
- ✪ Computer "superstores"
- ✪ Building supplies/hardware stores
- ✪ Gift and card shops

- Arts and crafts stores
- Toy or hobby stores
- Gag gift stores
- Health food/nutrition stores
- Bookstores
- Sports/athletic stores
- Pet stores
- Office supply stores
- High-tech/gadget stores
- Army/Navy stores
- Auto supply stores
- Music supply/record stores
- Graphic art stores

50. In what ways might you make your written sales proposals more:

- *Interesting to read? Examples:* Use of humor, cartoons, famous quotations, memorable metaphors.
- *Visually appealing on the outside and inside and "tastefully distinctive" compared to your competitors? Examples:* Special coverstock with pictures or custom prints, page layout design that makes it easier to read and for main points to "shout" at customer, use of colored, richly textured paper; an unusual size—larger or smaller or different shape as opposed to vertical format, special (but very readable) fonts.
- *Believable and overall persuasive? Examples:* Use of financial cost justification data using eye-catching pictographs, including a video of customer testimonials or clips of your product being used by customers.
- *Relevant to the prospect's needs and wants? Examples:* Use of realistic case studies highlighting your product's applications.

51. What colorful, descriptive language and terms can you think of to make your sales messages more powerful? What phrases and words would appeal to your customers' senses and make a purposeful psychological impact? How might you paint word pictures or situations that customers could "taste, smell, hear, see, and (most importantly) *emotionally feel?" Examples:*

"The stench of rotting corporate waste can be avoided with our new precision machinery." Or, "Our investment portfolio avoids your being on a perpetual exhausting emotional trampoline—endlessly and sometimes violently going up and down shaking your confidence as well as your bank account."

52. What technology trends should you be carefully watching into which you may tie your product or service solutions? How might you creatively take advantage of technological *change* better to meet the needs or solve problems of your customers?

53. What imaginative ideas can you think of to get an appointment with a very tough-to-"impossible"-to-see customer?

54. What are some poignant, compelling, and interest-sustaining ways to use financial cost justification techniques to help persuade customers of the attractive financial reasons to buy your product? For example, how can you make cost savings, return on investment (ROI), or payback clearly and impressively leap out at the prospect? How can you vividly show the financial superiority of your product or service solution compared to your competitors'?

55. How can your sales group transform themselves into an ongoing creative force? What types of policies, incentives, rewards, or awards (besides just monetary ones) would encourage salespeople in your group to use their creativity more? How can salespeople be given "amnesty" for trying some well-intentioned creative approaches that don't work out?

56. What helpful and unusual catalogs might you get ideas from or buy products (novelties, gifts, gags, props, games, or creative sales support materials) to use in your sales activities? Also, how might these catalog items be used in your office to create a playful environment? Here are a few diverse catalogs to consider:

* *Archie McPhee Outfitters of Popular Culture*, P.O. Box 30852, Seattle, WA 98103 (206-782-2344).
* *Brainstorms*, Division of Anatomical Chart Co., 8221 Kimball, Skokie, IL 60076-2956 (1-800-231-6000).
* *Edmund Scientific*, 101 E. Gloucester Pike, Barrington, NJ 08007-1380 (609-547-8880).

❧ *Flax Art and Design*, P.O. Box 7216, San Francisco, CA 94120-7216 (1-800-547-7778).

❧ *Gordons Wholesale Catalog*, Gordon's Novelty Company, 933 Broadway, New York, NY 10010 (212-254-8616(7)).

❧ *The Lighter Side*, 4514 19th Street Court East, P.O. Box 25600, Bradenton, FL 34206-5600 (813-747-2356).

❧ *The Mind's Eye*, Box 1060, Petaluma, CA 94953 (1-800-949-3333).

❧ *Performing Arts Catalog*, Norcostco, 3203 N. Highway 100, Minneapolis, MN 55422-2789 (612-533-2791).

❧ *Powerful Presentations*, Visual Horizons, 180 Metro Park, Rochester, NY 14623-2666 (716-424-5300).

❧ *The Sharper Image*, 650 Davis Street, San Francisco, CA 94111 (1-800-344-4444).

❧ *Things You Never Knew Existed . . .* , Johnson Smith Company, 4514 19th Street, P.O. Box 25500, Bradenton, FL 34206-5500 (813-747-2356).

❧ *Wireless*, Minnesota Public Radio, P.O. Box 64422, St. Paul, MN 55164-0422 (1-800-669-9999).

❧ *Worldwide Games*, P.O. Box 517, Colchester, CT 06415-0517 (1-800-888-0987).

57. How might you better use specialty preprinted papers (that can be printed from laser or inkjet printers) to better help you sell and service customers? These relatively inexpensive, quality-designed colored papers can be used for brochures, product specification sheets, testimonials, announcements, mailing labels, letterheads, certificates/awards, themes, business cards, tickets, newsletters, mailers, sales promotions, presentation kits, custom post/note cards, booklets, and other materials. Besides those, what other *new and creative uses* might you find for these attractive preprinted papers to be used with word processing and desktop publishing programs and copiers? Here are some companies to contact for catalogs of their paper and presentation products:

❧ *Baudville Desktop Publishing Solutions*, 5380 52nd Street S.E., Grand Rapids MI 49512-9765 (1-800-728-0888).

❧ *Image Street*, Moore Business Products Division, P.O. Box 5000, Vernon Hills, IL 60061 (1-800-462-4378).

⊛ *On Paper • The Image Authority*, P.O. Box 1365, Elk Grove Village, IL 60009-1365 (1-800-820-2299).

⊛ *Paper Design Warehouse*, 1720 Oak Street, Lakewood, NJ 08701 (1-800-836-5400).

⊛ *Paper Direct*, 100 Plaza Drive, Secaucus, NJ 07094-3606 (1-800-A-PAPERS).

⊛ *Premier Papers, Inc.*, P.O. Box 64785, St. Paul, MN 55164 (1-800-843-0414).

⊛ *Quill Laser and Inkjet Supplies*, 100 Schelter Road, Lincolnshire, IL 60069-3621 (1-800-789-5813).

⊛ *Quill Meeting and Presentation Solutions Catalog*, Schelter Road, Lincolnshire, IL 60069-3621 (708-634-4800).

⊛ *Wow! What a Great Presentation*, 100 Plaza Drive (2nd fl.), Secaucus, NJ 07094 (1-800-A-PAPERS).

58. How might you collaborate (in mutually beneficial ways) with local colleges, universities, or community colleges whereby competent and ambitious students can do real projects with your company and you'll obtain very inexpensive services while helping them out. For example, how might you use:

⊛ Art students to do graphic illustrations, cartoons, caricatures, desktop publishing, or electronic image manipulation for your extra creative sales projects?

⊛ Photography and videography students to create pictures and video for training, sales, and special customer presentations?

⊛ Media communications students to create multimedia and electronic slide programs?

⊛ Marketing students to do sales support activities to free up salespeople?

⊛ Architecture and interior design students to help redesign/redecorate your store, office, demo room, etc.?

59. What unconventional ways can you use more quickly, completely, and accurately to qualify your prospects—and do it in a way that's not obvious, manipulative, or pressure-prone?

60. How can you make your sales letters more concise, persuasive, visually attractive, attention-grabbing, and interest-holding? How can you use color, illustrations, pictures, scenes, inserts, photographs, or cartoons to liven them up visually? How can you

use the elements of curiosity, surprise, humor, challenge, reward, and "shocking" information to capture and hold the reader's attention? How about trying different paper sizes, textures, and colors to have a unique letter? What if your letter was round?

61. What really ingenious incentives or approaches might you use to help close more reluctant buyers? What could you do to reduce the apprehension of making a buying decision quickly?

62. How can you develop a more creative, more powerful competitive sales strategy? Consider these questions:

- In what ways can you better differentiate your company and its products and services from your competitors?
- What tough-to-get resources for implementing your strategy might you creatively obtain?
- In what ways can you dramatically highlight or amplify the value-added features of your products or services? How can you make *total value* seem overwhelmingly impressive?
- What can you do to confuse, bewilder, or jolt your competitor with an unexpected "brilliant" surprise course of action?
- What clever ways can you get your customer to feel a sense of urgency to go with your sales solution?
- How can you have satisfied customers, suppliers, and other "outsiders" help develop and implement/support your sales strategy?
- How can you creatively position your product's solutions in terms of amplifying their strengths/advantages and minimizing weaknesses compared to competitors? How can you make your product or service solution clearly and strongly appear to be the *best* solution available?
- What type of effective trap can you "bait" your competitors into?
- What "impenetrable" defensive tactics can you put in place before your competitor can attack?
- What single point of attack should you concentrate all your creative energy on to break into a competitor's stronghold?

⊛ How can you imaginatively escape "price wars" with your competitors or use them to your advantage?

⊛ What resourceful things can you do to prepare for and repel a competitive counterattack (even from several fronts)?

⊛ What can you do to add boldness, swiftness, and shrewdness to your strategies? (e.g., what might you do that would be uncharacteristic of past actions used by your sales organizations)?

⊛ How can you suddenly "change the ground rules" with your customer to knock your competitor off guard? For example, how can you creatively stall for time? Or, on what decision criteria can you try to change the emphasis?

63. When communicating to your customers at any point in the sales cycle, how can you make your information more interesting and more supportive of the key points you are making? For example, what analogies, assumptions, slogans, definitions, contrasts, comparisons, descriptions, anecdotes, quotations, references to magazine or newspaper articles, examples, explanations, facts, statistics, short stories, test reports, or other sources can you better use? How can you greatly amplify the impact of testimonials?

64. What fascinating trivia, eye-opening and eyebrow-raising facts, astonishing imponderables, surprising statistics, weird real-life stories, amusing situations/blunders, or otherwise unusual and entertaining information can you weave into your conversations, proposals, or formal sales presentations that will make your communication between you and your customer more interest-sustaining? How might you *poignantly and relevantly* tie that stuff to the points you're making? Following are types and examples of books that can help provide material for you (ask your librarian or bookstore clerk to give you other sources of interesting facts and stories):

⊛ *Isaac Asimov's Book of Facts* by Isaac Asimov
⊛ *The Blunder Book* by M. Hirsh Goldberg
⊛ *Big Secrets* by William Poundstone
⊛ *Do Penguins Have Knees?* by David Feldman
⊛ *One of a Kind* by Bruce Felton

⊕ *The Compass in Your Nose and Other Astonishing Facts About Humans* by Mark McCutcheon
⊕ *On an Average Day. . . .* by Tom Heymann
⊕ *News of the Weird* and *More News of the Weird* by Chuck Shepherd, John Kohut, and Roland Sweet

Another source of interesting tidbits that might prove useful is the *Harper's Index* from *Harper's* Magazine. Also, *The Funny Times, The Monthly Newspaper of Humor, Politics, and Fun* can be good sources of creative ideas (order a subscription from 2176 Lee Road, Cleveland, OH 44108; 216-371-8600).

65. What are some imaginative ways to get prospects to return your phone calls?

66. What are some unconventional ways to build powerful and lasting teamwork among your sales and service organization?

67. What ideas do you have to make your sales planning/forecasting process easier, faster, more complete, and more accurate?

68. How might you creatively use "inside salespeople" in your accounts to help you sell quicker and easier to others in the accounts?

69. How might your office be more attractively (and inexpensively) decorated to better impress customers?

70. What activities or sales situations might effectively lend themselves to using magic tricks or illusions? What key sales messages, objections, or competitive strongholds might magic illusions aid? Here are some resources to assist your sales organization in thinking about possible uses of magic for trade shows, large seminar selling presentations, promotional videos, or in other smaller, everyday ways:

⊕ *The Great American Masquerade Gag, Gift and Gadget Catalog* (134 pp.), Abracadabra, 10 Christopher Street, New York, NY 10014 (212-627-5745).
⊕ *Tannen's Catalog of Magic* (320 pp. of magic tricks, equipment, books, and effects), Louis Tannen, Inc., 6 W. 32nd St. (4th fl.), New York, NY 10001 (212-239-8383).
⊕ *Wellington Enterprises* provides design, engineering, craftsmanship, and essential services to assist users in ac-

complishing illusions of every kind before live audiences, as parts of shows, meetings, exhibits, and other performances. Contact William J. Schmeelk (owner), 55 Railroad Avenue, Building No. 5, Garnerville, NY 10923-0315 (914-429-3377).

71. What are the *two or three biggest problems* you or your sales group faces that would be ideal material for creative-thinking solutions?

72. What *two or three major opportunities* in your sales group or in your own selling situation might have a better chance of being taken advantage of if creative thinking were applied?

What are some other questions you can think of to apply creativity to in sales situations (write them below)?

73. _____

_____

_____

74. _____

_____

_____

75. _____

_____

_____

Pump 3:

Word-to-Idea Trigger List—A Useful Tool to Spark Your Imagination

The Word-to-Idea Trigger List that follows is a creative-thinking tool that expands beyond C.A.M.P.E.R. by giving you more words to create new possible connections to your ideas. The goal is to find a word that suddenly sparks an idea or creates a link between a problem you're facing and a solution you're seeking. Here's how it works: Scan through the groups of words without trying to think about anything. Some words or phrases will automatically begin shaping an idea for you or help to solve a problem. Just let your imagination roam freely as you go through the words in the category.

Combine

assortment	ensemble	integrate
blend	forge	join
brew	fuse	merge
centralize	hybrid	synthesize
composite	incorporate	unify

Reverse

180 degrees	converse	recycle
alternate	do the opposite	repel
backward	exchange	return
be contrary	inside out	turn back
by-pass	invert	upside down

Enlarge

add	exaggerate	make infinite
build up	expand	make longer
complement	increase	reproduce
deepen	intensify	strengthen
duplicate	magnify	stretch

Shrink

abbreviate	eliminate	squeeze
condense	lessen	streamline
contract	make smaller	subdue
decrease	purge	subtract
divide	reduce	understate

Substitute

commute	new approach	swap
find alternate	other location	transpose
how else?	replace	what else?
ingredient	stop gap	where else?
instead of	supplant	who else?

Sequence

break up	jump ahead	reorganize
by-pass	random	reschedule
cut in	rearrange	shuffle
disturb	reclassify	sort
interchange	regroup	vary

Modify

absorb	distort	new shape
accelerate	divide	overflow
add color	elevate	proportion
add flexibility	encircle	purify it
add functions	flatten	refine
add light	fold	revitalize
add motion	force fit	rip it
add precision	fuse	rotate it
add sound	inflate	separate it
add weight	intersect	sharpen
balance	magnetize	simplify
change altitude	magnitude	simulate
change flow	make pointed	soften
change pattern	make slippery	subdue
change rate	mask it	thicken
change scope	modularize it	tighten
change trend	multiply	tolerance
change volume	new attraction	transparent
decorate	new direction	twist
disintegrate	new packaging	vary rhythm

Action or Operation

absorb	impact	percentage
appreciate	impregnate	personify
attach	inquire	plant
bounce	joke	play
calculate	judge	pray
coordinate	jump	precaution
diagram	launch	prioritize
draw	levitate	profile
examine	limit	query
glide	link	quote
harmonize	list	react
hoist	locate	recede
hook	loosen	recruit
hover	mediate	satiate
idle	mimic	scrutinize
ignite	miracle	stage
illuminate	outline	trigger
illustrate	pain	volatile
imagine	pause	weigh
immerse	pendulum	whirl

Strategy

abandon	goodwill	pardon
accelerate	icebreaker	parody
advance	incentive	parry
attract	indirect	partner
be bold	involve	phase-in
beautify	isolate	ploy
captivate	liberate	preserve
confine	maintain	provocative
confuse	marathon	puzzle
contact	mock	radical
contradict	monopolize	rectify
controversial	myth	sacrifice
create illusion	negotiate	scale back
debate	obstruct	scare
deprive	oppose	share

diversify	option	spoof
entertain	overwhelm	surprise
facade	pacify	surround
fantasy	parable	understate
force	paradox	wear down

Quality/Trait/Description

abundant	conservative	gullible
agile	cunning	idealistic
airy	curious	imaginative
alert	daring	infallible
amusing	decisive	infinite
bewildering	diplomatic	inquiring
bold	enjoyable	intimate
brilliant	euphoric	intricate
cautious	excitable	kink
charming	exhilarating	lax
classical	expressive	loyal
colorless	festive	luxurious
comical	flirtatious	
compulsive	generous	

There are two very useful idea-generating and organizing software programs (run on Macintosh and IBM-compatible systems) that you might consider using on a regular basis.

Ideafisher™ is a simple-to-use and powerful program focusing on the principles of association, memory retrieval, and analogical reasoning (use of analogy and metaphor). It contains nearly 6,000 organized questions and over 61,000 organized idea words that provide more than 700,000 associated links. That means you have seemingly unlimited ways of making new idea connections. Contact: Ideafisher Systems, Inc., 2222 Martin Street, Suite 110, Irvine, CA 92715 (714 474-8111).

Inspiration™ is based upon the concepts of mind mapping, clustering, and idea mapping and can help you brainstorm, diagram, and organize ideas very effectively. Contact: Inspiration Software, Inc., P.O. Box 1629, Portland, OR 97207 (503 245-9011).

Pump 4:
Fun and Play at Work—Checklist
of 100 Ideas to Amuse and Use

Browse through the following checklist for ideas on how you, your co-workers, and managers can create a work climate that has more fun, merriment, and satisfaction to it. Also, develop your own thoughts. Remember that creativity blooms in a work environment where stress is low and appropriate diversion exists. We've attempted to offer a wide range of ideas, from those that are very "practical" to those that border on the silly side of the idea spectrum. You may need to tone down some aspects of them for your organization's work culture. Or, if your workplace is kind of "wild and crazy" to begin with, your group may even decide to crank up some of these ideas into the realm of *The Twilight Zone!* Either way, we hope you get enough ideas to use in whatever form you decide is helpful.

1. Organize a brainstorming session to gather ideas on how to put more fun, merriment, and play into your workplace. Then, *implement* the best ideas quickly.

2. Take video movies at work. Use amusing narrations or make it into a "spoof" documentary or television show format.

3. Organize potluck lunches.

4. Have everyone chip in to hire a professional masseuse.

5. Have a "brainteaser contest" with several tough puzzles to solve. Give out novel prizes to the winners.

6. Give your meeting rooms interesting and inspiring/cute names such as "Imagination Den," "Idea Haven," "The Brain Room," "Innovation Sanctum," or "Creativity Cave." Spruce them up with funny pictures, neat posters, and other things.

7. Make up silly acronyms for annoying rules, constricting policies, or stifling political situations.

8. Have a manager's barbecue picnic where they cook and serve employees (no pun intended!).

9. Have popcorn at meetings. Have popcorn breaks. Put a popcorn machine in the office. Have a popcorn arts and crafts contest. Have a popcorn-throwing fight.

10. Have a morning and afternoon ten-minute easy aerobic or Yoga exercise break.

11. Regularly post several cartoons on the bulletin board. Have a running contest where employees fill in captions. Give prizes for the best one for each cartoon.

12. Create a series of monthly or quarterly awards, e.g., "most patient employee," "most imaginative," "most daring," "most outrageous," "most humorous."

13. Have a contest for most interesting T-shirt, classiest shoes, loudest tie, coolest hat, most colorful nails, most changed hairdo.

14. Have a "make up the wildest story" contest.

15. Have people bring in baby pictures of themselves. Have a contest for the "cutest," "funniest," "most mature looking," "most serious."

16. In the department newsletter, include a column for people to volunteer their "most embarrassing moment."

17. Have a stand-up comedy day at lunch. Have employees volunteer or ask aspiring comics to come in and test their routines out. Have "best" and "worst" awards and the "best of the worst."

18. Create a bumper sticker slogan day. Ask people to submit serious or funny sayings about anything. Publish the best ten in your newsletter or post them on the bulletin board. Or, make up bumper stickers for people to use on their vehicles.

19. Have "category joke" days. Ask people to submit a joke about a particular topic.

20. Create a "Jeopardy"-type game with work-related categories/questions. Give prizes. Make it a fun, but also a *learning* experience!

21. Have raffles or lotteries with various prizes. Use the money to improve something for employees.

22. Print out funny sayings on computer banner paper and hang them up.

23. Present "You Walk On Water" certificates to employees who did an outstanding job or took an initiative to solve a problem.

24. Have a "nickname party." Ask people to submit catchy (positive, cute, or complimentary) nicknames for each other. Use them at special times.

25. Organize work-related "mini-Olympics" where teams compete against each other in various work-related tasks, e.g. fastest team typing time, memory test, parts assembly.

26. Run a game-of-the-month contest such as Trivial Pursuit, Monopoly, chess, or checkers.

27. Play physical skill games, e.g., tossing, throwing, placing, that can be played in a team way. Give best and worst score prizes.

28. Make up funny Murphy's laws that apply to your company and workplace.

29. Have people create a *Guinness Book of World Records* about people's performance or lack thereof (fictitious names) and related company operations.

30. Hold a lottery: three to four winners get treated to a lunch or dinner with important managers.

31. Replace common acronyms used in your workgroup with funny ones.

32. Create a company recipe book with names such as "Humble Pie," "Management Mush, " "Fruitcake Idea," "Eating Crow," "Suffering Succotash," "Situation Stew," and "Leg of Lame (excuse)."

33. Have a company talent show.

34. Get a group together to write a company jingle or outrageous radio commercial.

35. Switch popular advertising slogans to apply to your company or workplace.

36. Have a toilet paper unrolling/rerolling contest with quickest times garnering the coveted "John Award."

37. Run a contest for the funniest employee home video.

38. Create a sticker system. Every time someone does you a favor, they get a sticker. They can be cashed in for prizes when people accumulate enough.

39. Add a section of funny quotes to the company or department newsletter.

40. Have a Karioke singing contest with individual and group singoffs. Make up new words to songs.

41. Hold a "best excuse for screwing up" contest.

42. Have people who are on vacation or out of town send in the weirdest postcards they can find. Put them on the bulletin board.

43. Create a set of funny rubber stamps for everyone to use for feedback and instructions. *Example:* If you review a memo and approve, it gets a smiley face stamp.

44. Have guessing contests with prizes, things like how many beans in the jar, the weight of some object, the middle name of the boss's spouse.

45. Create games that mimic those on television but with funny names like the "Wheel of Misfortune," "Department Feud," "The Price Isn't Right."

46. Have a kazoo, harmonica, and jew's harp playoff.

47. Come up with some wacky titles of possible books that could be written about your workplace culture and situations.

48. Get a group of people to go to a big toy store for ideas and buy some fun things to use or display at work.

49. Create a parody chain letter in your workplace that's tailored to your company and industry. *Example:* "A good quarter will come to those who don't break the chain. Someone who broke the chain within a week had all his vacation luggage sent to Bulgaria instead of Hawaii."

50. Create a year-end award contest that simulates the Academy Awards with honors going to "best performance,"

"sharpest idea," "most courageous effort," "most unusual special effects," "best costumes," and also some other fun categories.

51. Have a funny quotation, joke, or saying-of-the-day to accompany E-mail messages.

52. Make up impressive-sounding funny jargon that has absolutely no real meaning.

53. Do a work-related takeoff of David Letterman's "Top Ten List."

54. Write a weekly or monthly Dear Abby-type column. Call it something like "Dear Bertha." Make up crazy problems people have and give outrageous answers.

55. Make up silly variations of famous quotes and put them on the top or bottom of memos. *Example:* "Look before you leap. But don't take a leap in my office."

56. Using popular computer software programs, create greeting cards, signs, and company-customized calendars using cartoon clipart.

57. Have a complete-the-sentence contest. Have people reach in a bowl and pull out a folded piece of paper with such phrases as, "People say I'm good-looking because . . ." or "If I were a food, I'd be . . ."

58. Hire a caricaturist to come into the office.

59. Put in volleyball, shuffleboard, basketball courts. Consider a polo field if yours is a high-brow type company (sure . . . !).

60. Have hula-hoop contests—longest duration and greatest number of simultaneous hoops going at once.

61. Teach juggling and use it as a metaphor for learning to do many things at once without "dropping anything."

62. Put in a large fish tank at work. Have a "name-the-fish" or "adopt-a-fish" qualification contest.

63. Let people creatively decorate their offices any way they want (minus, of course, any offensive or otherwise unprofessional stuff).

64. Have an April Fool's Day each quarter with planned activities.

65. Make a "field trip" to a comedy club. Have a meeting the next day to actually see if anyone got any creative ideas to somehow use.

66. Once a month, have a fun collective birthday party for those who had one during that month. Call them "mirthday events."

67. Do a light-hearted videotape "news program" using a home video format. Enlist the help of journalism students at a nearby college as a way of doing a project. Give personal news and interviews with employees who were recently married, made new parents, went on vacation, or received some award or other recognition or accomplishment.

68. Have a department walkathon. Sing or do funny cadence calls while walking.

69. Make up a spoof "gossip" magazine of your company or department. Call it something like the *National Inquisitor (Exhibitor, Excelsior,* etc.). Make up crazy stories, e.g., alien abduction of certain employees, a fake gossip column, wild predictions for the year by a company seer.

70. Plant a botanical garden of "interesting" plastic plants in your office and water them while people are there.

71. Ask employees to do amusing skits during training events relating to the topics they are learning. Give out prizes for the most outrageous, amusing, accurate, etc.

72. Have a carnival. Put in rides and game booths at your company for a day or two.

73. Have employees write a hilarious "soap opera" script. Create a videotape and rename the program after a major soap such as "As the Division Turns" or "The Old and the Restless." Make light of everyday plots, crises, relationships, and experiences.

74. Encourage volunteers to do a funny two-minute monologue at the beginning of the monthly meeting.

75. Have a group barbecue in the parking lot.

76. Design a friendly animal cartoon mascot for your company. Give it a "catchy" name like "Cedric the Seal," "Rupert Armadillo," "Archibald Owl," or "Gotcha Goat."

77. Get your work teams to compete in a canoeing race in a nearby big pond or lake. Getting people to try to row together in some coherent way is not only a good team metaphor, but will elicit huge laughs and long-term remembrance chuckles.

78. Have an art exhibit day to show off employees' paintings, photographs, sculptures, arts and crafts, or handiwork. Give prizes for the two best in each category.

79. Ask employees to come up with "new" business cards. Have them think of amusing, but still somewhat relevant titles, name changes, and slogans or other laughable information that might be included on the card. *Examples:* "Sales Emperor," "Assistant Service Swami," "Brilliant Problem Solver," or "Director of Creative Misfits."

80. Design a wacky room solely for the purpose of light-years-out creative thinking and problem solving. Decorate it such that people naturally lose their uptight inhibitions once they're inside. We've heard rumors about think-rooms with a grass-thatched bar stocked with soft drinks/juices, raised toilet bowls as seats, and a wise-cracking chicken (a la Groucho Marx's duck on "You Bet Your Life" TV show) that is electrically lowered from the ceiling when someone presses a button.

81. Have people compete to come up with the toughest and most creative work-related tongue-twisters.

82. Have a timed event called something like the "Mine Fine Whine Time." The goal is facetiously to whine about small problems at work without stopping between sentences (breathing is optional!). Whoever lasts longest in a continuous *w-h-i-n-e* wins a bottle of wine.

83. Put in ping-pong tables (inside or outside).

84. Have team rope-pulling contests where teams of four to six grab opposing ends of a heavy duty rope and try to pull the other team over a line, a puddle of water, etc. Wear gloves and don't strain yourselves!

85. Have a poetry runoff where employees make up amusing, satirical poems about work.

86. Have a birthday candle blowing contest where teams of three compete. The ones who can extinguish the most candles in one continuous breath win the "Grand Blowhard Award."

87. Play charades with work-related phrases, themes, and titles.

88. Have an "articulation test" in which contestants read a complex paragraph *backwards.* The one who does it the fastest with fewest mistakes wins.

89. Run an essay contest called "Why I Love My Boss." Embellishing details, stretching the truth, pontificating, and using other humorous good-natured portrayals should be encouraged.

90. Have brainstorming sessions focusing on office design improvements where people suggest ways to decorate/redesign the office in more festive, friendly, and personal ways.

91. Program your company's networked computers to have cartoon characters greet employees with a funny saying each day they start up their computers.

92. Have free lollipops in the office. There's nothing quite so unintimidating as seeing the boss with one. Be a sucker for fun!

93. In one of the meeting rooms used for creative brainstorming, ask employees to design a "graffiti wall" on which they write or spray paint clever sayings.

94. As a takeoff on the national shouting contests in the United States and Japan, for example, have a *Sales Message Shouting Contest* as a very amusing exercise that also relieves stress during a big (quarterly or annual) sales meeting. Ask people to shout a five- or ten-second sales messages (they create) as loud as they can. Buy a sound (decibel measuring) meter from a store like Radio Shack and record the levels of everyone. Give prizes to the top three "big mouths." *Caution:* Check with a throat doctor beforehand to give warnings and suggestions on proper technique.

95. Create an award called something like "The Motivated

Maverick," "The Responsible Rebel," or "The Conscientious Contrarian," for example. The award is given to those hardy, brave souls who came with a bright (but tough-to-sell) idea and stuck to their guns to implement it by cleverly and professionally getting around the stifling, crazy, and restrictive rules of your company's bureaucracy and politics.

96. Have teams compete in crossword puzzle contests.

97. Get teams to compete in a simple and fun innovation contest. Give it a name like "Higher Up Smarts." Give each team (of three to four) persons 150 wooden popsicle sticks, 45 paper clips, and a hot glue gun. The goal is to build the tallest structure that can remain standing. Tell teams you will let them try three times using 50 sticks and any number of paper clips each try (they should learn and get better from every attempt). Then discuss *what* they learned, *how* they learned from mistakes, and *how they can apply* those learning-type mistakes to improve their jobs. Give out prizes to each team with categories like "tallest structure," "most unusual design," and "most stable." Make everyone feel as if he or she accomplished something and learned from it.

98. Have teams write up and read (with theatrical enthusiasm) the wildest and craziest telephone answering message for the department contest.

99. On the bulletin board or in your organization's newsletter, include an entertaining section, "What Our Kids Will Say!" Include those cherishing, amusing, and wildly imaginative things said by one's child, grandchild, niece/nephew, etc.

100. Have a contest to make up the most exotic, bizarre, and laughable names for new women's and men's colognes.

Below, write down *your* ideas to put more fun, play, relaxation, and joy into your work environment:

1. _____

_____

_____

2. _____

_____

_____

3. _____

_____

_____

4. _____

_____

_____

Pump 5:
Book List—Suggested Reading

The following pages list books on creativity, humor, problem solving, and other related topics to enable you to expand your knowledge base.

Adams, James L. *Conceptual Blockbusting, 3rd Ed.* Reading, Mass.: Addison-Wesley, 1986.

Agor, Weston. *Intuitive Management.* Englewood Cliffs, N.J.: Prentice-Hall, 1984.

Blohowiak, Donald W. *Mavericks! How to Lead Your Staff to Think Like Einstein, Create Like da Vinci, and Invent Like Edison.* Homewood, Ill.: Business One Irwin, 1992.

Bransford, John D., and Barry S. Stein. *The Ideal Problem Solver.* New York: W. H. Freeman and Company, 1984.

Carr, Clay. *The Power of Constant Creativity.* New York: AMACOM, 1994.

Chaffee, J. *Thinking Critically.* Boston: Houghton Mifflin, 1985.

Clark, Charles. *Idea Management: How to Motivate Creativity and Innovation.* New York: AMACOM, 1980.

DeBono, Edward. *Serious Creativity.* New York: HarperCollins, 1992.

DeBono, Edward. *Six Action Shoes.* New York: HarperBusiness, 1991.

Fagan, Pete. *The Office Humor Book*. New York: Crown Publishers, 1985.

Farber, Barry J., and Joyce Wycoff. *Breakthrough Selling*. Englewood Cliffs, N.J.: Prentice-Hall, 1992.

Garfield, Patricia. *Creative Dreaming*. New York: Random House, 1976.

Glanz, Barbara A. *The Creative Communicator: 399 Tools to Communicate Commitment Without Boring People to Death!* Homewood, Illinois: Business One Irwin, 1993.

Goleman, Daniel, Paul Kaufman, and Michael Ray. *The Creative Spirit*. New York: Dutton, 1992.

Gross, T. Scott. *Positively Outrageous Service. New and Easy Ways to Win Customers for Life*. New York: Mastermedia, 1991.

Hayes, J. R. *The Complete Problem Solver*. Philadelphia: Franklin Institute Press, 1981.

Helmstetter, Shad. *You Can Excel in Times of Change.* New York: Pocket Books, 1991.

Hillkirk, John, and Gary Jacobson. *Grit, Guts, and Genius. True Tales of Megasuccess*. Boston: Houghton Mifflin, 1990.

Keil, J. M. *The Creative Mystique: How to Manage It, Nurture It, and Make It Pay.* New York: John Wiley & Sons, 1985.

Kushner, Malcolm. *The Light Touch. How to Use Humor For Business Success*. New York: Simon & Schuster, 1990.

LeBoeuf, Michael. *Imagineering*. New York: McGraw-Hill, 1984.

MacCrimmon, Kenneth R., and Donald A. Wehrung. *Taking Risks. The Management of Uncertainty*. New York: Free Press, 1986.

Mansfield, R., and T. Busse. *The Psychology of Creativity and Discovery*. Chicago: Nelson-Hall, 1981.

May, Rollo. *The Courage to Create*. New York: W. W. Norton and Company, 1975.

Mayer, R. E. *Thinking, Problem Solving, Cognition*. New York: W. H. Freeman, 1983.

Moore, L. P. *You're Smarter Than You Think: At Least 500 Fun Ways to Expand Your Own Intelligence.* New York: Holt, Rinehart & Winston, 1984.

Morris, Jim. *Creative Breakthroughs. Tap the Power of Your Unconscious Mind*. New York: Warner Books, 1992.

Murphy, Joseph. *The Power of Your Subconscious Mind*. New York: Bantam, 1982.

Osborn, Alex. *How to Become More Creative: 101 Rewarding Ways to Develop Your Potential Talent.* New York: Charles Scribner's Sons, 1964.

Ray, Michael, and Rochelle Myers. *Creativity in Business.* New York: Doubleday, 1986.

Rubinstein, M. F., and K. Pfeiffer. *Concepts in Problem Solving.* Englewood Cliffs, N.J.: Prentice-Hall, 1980.

Ruchlis, Hy. *Clear Thinking.* New York: Prometheus Books, 1990.

Schwartz, David J. The Magic of Thinking Big. New York: Fireside, 1987.

Sinetar, Marsha. *Developing a 21st Century Mind.* New York: Villard Books, 1991.

Sloane, Paul. *Lateral Thinking Puzzlers.* New York: Sterling, 1991.

Springer Sally P., and Georg Deutsch. *Left Brain, Right Brain.* New York: W. H. Freeman and Company, 1985.

Thompson, Charles. *What a Great Idea! The Key Steps Creative People Take.* New York: HarperCollins, 1992.

VanGrundy, Arthur. *Managing Group Creativity.* New York: AMACOM, 1984.

VanGrundy, Arthur. *108 Ways to Get a Bright Idea and Increase Your Creative Potential.* Englewood Cliffs, N.J.: Prentice-Hall, 1984.

Waitley, Denis E., and Robert B. Ticker. *Winning the Innovation Game.* New York: Berkley, 1989.

Weinberg, R. *Creativity: Genius and Other Myths.* New York: W. H. Freeman, 1986.

Wilson, Steve. *The Art of Mixing Work and Play.* Columbus, Ohio: Ohio Professional Counseling Services, Inc. 1992.

Winter, Arthur and Ruth Winter. *Build Your Brain Power.* New York: St. Martin's, 1986.

Wycoff, Joyce. *Mindmapping.* New York: Berkley, 1991.